Dedication and Thanks

This book is dedicated to my family, who without them, most of these stories would not have been possible.

Russian Proverb: "Usually with age comes wisdom, but sometimes age comes alone"

© 11/30/20 by Paul Fuquer

ISBN: 978-0-9798563-2-7

The "Letter Guy" and Other Stories

Table of Contents

The "Letter Guy" and Other Stories

Why Write This Book?   1-

A good question. "Why not?" I guess you could also ask. After years of regaling people with apparently "normal" childhoods with stories from my childhood, it became obvious to me that I somehow grew up in a far more exciting, yet sinister place, filled with intrigues and dirty tricks. A place where one's greatest pleasure was to see one's adversary psychologically tormented; caught in some elaborate trap. It was only after years of telling these stories to others that I realized that "there may be gold in them thar hills" and that people may actually pay money to read about the stuff we did to each other, those closest to us, and any innocent bystanders that happened into our sphere.

So, without further ado, let's embark on a humourous, but pointless voyage through my past . . .

The "Letter Guy" and Other Stories

2.1 My Brother - Dave Fuquer

Since I'm writing this part, I get to pull the mask off my brother and expose him for who he really is: the enemy.

My earliest memory of David happened when I was coming up on 3 years old. Mom had been really packing on the weight recently and had developed a large belly. Since I was already becoming the charming, discrete gentleman that all knew and loved, I knew enough to keep my mouth shut and not say anything to her about her weight problem. However, as it turned out, she was the one who broached the subject with me.

"Put your hand on my tummy," Mom said to me one afternoon in her bedroom. Dutifully I placed my hand on her tummy and wondered where the hell she was going with this. "You're going to have a brother, and he's in here," she said, eyes beaming with happiness. Or maybe, just maybe, that wasn't happiness in her eyes, but wistfulness. Regret. The knowledge that by getting herself knocked up, she had ruined the perfect time when there was only me - her firstborn. The love of her life - Paul. Paul The Magnificent. Paul The Great.

My eyes glazed over. "Blah, blah, blah . . ." Mom prattled on about some crap involving the advent of David. Meanwhile, I had to get out of there and play. I had no time to waste on some conversation about a brother. I didn't need one, and sure as hell didn't want one.

That's it. That's the only memory I have of David until I hit 6 years old. Everything else about my brother (who obviously lived with us during this time) is a blank. I'm told

3

that I used to mess with him a little bit, but nothing significant. For instance, here is one story, that when I heard it recounted to me brought back a little piece of David in my early life:

Story #1: Tricycles and The Furnace

We grew up in this small, one-story house in Ottawa, Canada that was basically two single-wide trailers bolted together on top of an unfinished basement. In the far corner of the basement was a smelly oil tank, and a forced air furnace. Being an unfinished basement, there were a couple of bare 3 Watt light bulbs that gave the dark a yellowish tinge when they were turned on, but that was about it.

Needless to say, the scariest, darkest place in our house was behind the furnace.So (yes you guessed it) - that's where I used to try and trap Dave.

Part of the reason I hated Dave so much as a kid, was that he was always following me around, trying to get half of everything my parents dished out, and basically being uncool and a baby. It drove me mental. However, I was able to sometimes utilize his "Paul fixation" to his own undoing.

For instance, we both had tricycles in the basement (it was Canada - if you went outside, you'd freeze to death, if the wolves didn't get you first[†]). Hence the Syrian dungeon of a kids play-area in the basement. Now, back to the story.

Apparently, Dave liked to follow me around in the basement on his tricycle, but had issues with going

---

[†] This is poetic license to offend any Canadians who may be reading this book.

backwards. So, what I'd do is lead him on a merry chase: around the jack-post in the center of the basement a couple of times, over to the wringer-washer, back to the jack-post, and then off to the scary realm behind the furnace, where - lo and behold - my tricycle would break down, leaving Dave trapped behind the furnace.

Since reverse on Dave's tricycle didn't work, I'd have to take off, leaving him wailing for help, as I wandered off upstairs. (What would have been really great would have been to shut off the lights and leave, but I don't think I could reach the pull cords on the two lights).

Regardless, Mom would eventually drag herself downstairs to save her demon-spawn, and then I'd have to concoct some story about how my tricycle got stuck, and that I hadn't really wanted to abandon Dave behind the furnace.

Maybe she bought it the first time (and maybe not), but it didn't take many more of these "my tricycle got stuck" episodes to earn me a spanking.

2.2 My Father - Edwin

Dad, when he wasn't being serious and/or spanking me for some misdeed, was essentially like an older brother, partaking equally in many of Dave's and my psychological wars, and regaling us with stories and stunts from his youth. He did so many cool things, that I remember consciously thinking in Grade 2 that I had better start doing some stuff, or I'd have no stories at all in my life. He'd blown up the family toaster by putting tire chains in it,[†] shot .22 longs through the outhouse door in his backyard,

---

[†] OK - I found out it was actually his brother that did it, but the effect was the same

thrown fire-wood onto his neighbour's roof - all sorts of ultra-cool stuff! He was my role model.

He was also essential to our psychological wars, as if Dad was involved, we were basically immune from any really serious punishment. If he wasn't, then things were a lot more dicey - sometimes you got a spanking, other times just got a lecture and sent to your room.

2.3 My Mother - Leone

Mom basically had no sense of humour. For her, raising my brother and I, (and to some extent my Dad) was one long death-march of unappreciated cooking and silly childish activity at the dinner table. No sooner did we wolf the food down that she had prepared, than we'd bolt from the dinner table to go play (or in later years to watch TV - something that prior to getting a color TV and cable in Canada was useless). Dad would always do the dishes, so it wasn't like Ma shouldered the entire burden of domestic bliss all by herself. But it was essentially like cooking for Klingons.

Needless to say, Mom was the perfect foil for our family comedy. The pained looks of disgust and disappointment that crossed her face upon witnessing us in action were priceless. All we had to do was make sure that nothing actually happened to her. Because if it did - the party was over.

2.4 The Cat - Shadow

Shadow (aka Cat - no "the" - just Cat) was the coolest member of our family, and was the person (OK, cat) that my brother and I most looked up to. She walked proud, didn't take crap from anybody, and basically did her own thing. Naturally she was a target for psychological torture as well, and hence her inclusion in the list of players.

Figure 2.1 **Cat**

2.5 Me - Paul

OK - so I'm going to have to write this on behalf of my brother, whom I'm sure has some less-than-pleasant things to say about me, but if I can get to my "imperfections" first, perhaps I will be able to paint them in a more forgiving light. Yeah - whatever . . .

So - I am a caring, giving, sort of person who enjoys nothing more than helping others, and performing selfless acts of philanthropy. During my many years of being a live-in older brother, and care-giver to my younger brother, I tirelessly strove to help both him and my parents in life. Whether it was just that little extra touch of getting up at 4:00am to polish my Mom's silverware, or something as simple as fluffing my brother's pillow for him before going to bed, I thrived on the quiet knowledge that I had bettered my family's life and that was enough for me.

OK - that's it. No more introductions until much later - we're done, class is dismissed. So without further ado, let's get down to some stories.

Since I just finished telling you that I didn't remember jack about my brother from before I was six, I'm obviously going to start there.

Story #2: The Eraser

Somewhere around Grade 1, I figured out two things:

1) Any time I got something cool, my whining, weasel of a brother would kick up a fuss, and Mom and Dad would give him the same thing. It didn't matter if it was collecting stamps, crap from a cereal box, or whatever: Dave always got what I got.

   I hated it. Being a competitive bastard, this basically meant that even when I showed initiative and did something, he'd always horn in on the action.

2) The young Dave (i.e., 3-4 years old) was really dopey, and you could trade just about any piece of garbage for his half of the goods. I quickly figured this out, and started methodically cleaning out his stash of goodies in exchange for old bottle caps, rocks I'd picked up on the way home from school, etc. Basically pretty much anything would work as long as you could fake that you thought it was cool, and had value. Even my best friend at school, Dietmar, got in on the act, trading crap for Dave's stamps, etc. Here's an example of the dialog we used on Dave:

   (Paul and Dietmar enter holding a couple of pieces of gray gravel. Dave is busy doing whatever the hell Dave did with himself at that point in his life. Don't ask me, I have no memory of what he did for amusement. He

9

could have been flying around the room for all I cared . . .)

PAUL: "Wow Dietmar - this is sure one cool rock!"

DIETMAR: "Yeah. It's sooo cool. I sure wish I could have it!"

PAUL: "Naw - I want this for my collection. Nobody has a rock like this!"

(Dave perks up and wanders over to look at the rock)

DAVE: "Paul - can I see it? Can I?"

PAUL: "Go away - it's mine! *(Even though the rock is worthless, it makes it even sweeter to make him beg for a look at it!)*"

DAVE: "Mom! Paul won't show me his rock!"

Mom: "Paul - show your brother your stupid rock!!"

(Paul "reluctantly" reveals his "treasure" to an eager David)

DAVE: "Wow! Can I have it?"

DIETMAR: "No way! If anybody is going to get it, I am"

DAVE: "Please?"

PAUL: "Well - if you were willing to give me something really cool back, maybe you could have it"

DIETMAR: "Oh no! Don't do it! That rock's way too cool to trade!"

DAVE: "Please?"

PAUL: "I don't know . . . What about the eraser? Do you still have that old thing?"

Unfortunately, Dietmar's involvement was the undoing of the whole thing, as one day Mom wondered why the hell Dietmar would ever care to talk to my brother, or give him anything. A quick interrogation of Dave revealed that 3 - 4 years of valuables were now in the possession of Paul and his evil friend. Promptly, all of the great trades were undone, including the trade of all trades: a piece of gravel for a pastel eraser - identical to the one I got for Christmas, except a different color. These erasers, for some God-unbeknownest reason, were the penultimate prizes in Dave's and my collections. They were made of a semi-translucent material and colored in a pleasant pastel shade, and each came with a matching, soft plastic holder. I recall that one was blue, though at this point I can't even tell you which one of us was the original recipient of this treasure. The color of the other one escapes me. Something like yellow or pink. I'm sure my rat-bastard brother remembers. Ask him. He even probably has his eraser locked up in a bank-vault somewhere - along with mine, which I haven't been able to locate for years!

Story #3: The Eraser War

Anyway - these erasers became the prizes in a decade-long war in which the goal was to seize the other's eraser. It began the minute my brother realized that wonderful, caring Paul was actually cheating him out of his stuff, and that what I wanted most of all in the world was his stupid eraser. I still remember seeing that newly dawned, feral light in his eyes as his hands closed around his unjustly returned eraser - the sickening look of triumph

on his face - gloating, mocking. Thus began the eraser war.

Initially, the war consisted primarily of waiting until the other one was away and then making forays into the other's room to root around obvious hiding places to find the secreted eraser. For me it was particularly easy to find my brother's eraser, as his idea of hiding something when he was three years old was pretty ridiculous. Usually he just stuffed the eraser under some crap, imagining somehow that I wouldn't look underneath, and then presto, the eraser was back in its rightful owner's possession. I on the other hand would hide my eraser under the drawers in my dresser, or secrete it on a ledge under my boxspring bed. OK - so none of this was exactly "protect state secrets" grade security, but for my younger brother it was more than sufficient to baffle him. Hence in the eraser war, I would usually be able to quickly locate my brother's eraser, whereas he would usually come away empty-handed from forays into my room.

Unfortunately, this happy state of affairs lasted only until Dave decided to go and view his stupid eraser and discover that it wasn't there. Sometimes several weeks could go by before Dave discovered that his prized possession was gone. Especially if I had let a month or so pass between repatriation events, and he would get tired of checking that "his" eraser was still there.

Inevitably though, he'd check, and there'd follow the standard "Mom! Paul took my eraser!" Now I was always the paragon of truth, but when my nasty brother ratted me out to the authorities, I would be forced to lie that I had no knowledge of any eraser, and that David was probably just a little delusional. This then led to Mom threatening me with the wooden spoon, or some other medieval torture, which (like waterboarding) quickly led to a confession from

me, more gloating from David, and immediate plans by me to swipe the eraser again.[†]

Story #4: The Safe

These incursions into each other's room continued for some period of time until I decided that I had enough of Dave stealing my stuff, and decided to build myself a little safe. My Dad had been doing some sort of renovation to our kitchen that involved pulling off a charming little divider between our back door and the kitchen that was made of 3/4" plywood painted a lovely pastel lime color.[‡] Suddenly, I had the material that I needed. With some minor help from my Dad (OK - so when I look at the safe now, it is pretty clear that Dad basically built it), I cranked together a 1' cube of 3/4" plywood with an inset door on hinges, a hasp, and a little pad-lock. Nirvana! Finally my stuff would be safe from Dave!![*]

Dad at the time was feeling a "father-and-son"-like pride as he helped his little boy construct something that he had designed. This happy state of affairs did not continue very long[††] before Dave was whining and moaning that he needed a safe too, and it wasn't fair that Paul got one, and he didn't. I remember Dad saying that he'd help Dave build one, if Dave designed it, and helped, but considering that Dave could barely draw, the chances of this happening

---

[†] Geez - in recounting this tale, it isn't clear to me how often Dave ever even got my eraser. However, I have memory of him having touched mine once, so I think it is more than fair to refer to both sides as aggressors.

[‡] What the hell were people thinking in the late sixties????

[*] More like "Now I could steal his stuff, and he couldn't get it back without whining to our parents" . . .

[††] OK - it was probably a couple of hours. Perhaps it was my shoving his nose in it, and capering about teasing him that I had a safe now and he didn't, and that he was a loser, etc.

Plate 3.1 **The safe - now residing in my attic**

were zero. Impervious to my pleas, Mom made Dad make Dave a copy of my safe, so that now we both had one. So there we were in an arms race - both of us with safes, both containing our erasers and other "treasures." So - what happened next? We now had to find the key to the other's safe, or, as I discovered later, you could just get a #0 Phillips screwdriver and take the hasp off.

Story #5: Stickers

The second-most valued prizes in our possession were a set of ridiculous "Tony-The-Tiger" Cities of the World stickers that came in what (obviously) had to be "Frosted Flakes" cereal boxes. These prizes would live somewhere in the cereal, and as soon as a new box would show up, we would dig like frantic gophers into the cereal, distending

the box so that it would no longer close. Things even got to such a state that the infamous cereal-box law was enacted which forbade digging for prizes until they "naturally" fell out. Yeah, right . . . Anyways, back to the stickers.

I started collecting these, and immediately Dave wanted in on the action. So Mom was forced to Solomonically divide the stickers up between us. This proceeded fine, with doubles happily occurring, until one fateful morning when either a Paris or Rio (I don't remember which) singleton showed up. Both of us "needed" this for our collection, and of course, Mom mistakenly gave the crown-jewel of my sticker collection to my arch-rival David. I of course, at the earliest opportunity, peeled the sticker off his desk (where his collection was proudly displayed) and stuck it on my dresser, admiring the completeness of my collection - the sheer symmetrical perfection of it. Unfortunately Dave came home, and once again, the party was over.

"Mom! Paul took my sticker!" yelled Dave.

I begged, pleaded, whined, promised other future stickers, viewing privileges of the current relocated sticker, showed how the sticker would clearly never survive being re-peeled off my dresser, and that in the name of all that was good and decent in the world, the sticker should just be left alone on my dresser. No dice. Off came the sticker, and back into David's hovel it went, where the little jerk proceeded to tape it to his desk, forever ruining the integrity, and hence the street-value, of the sticker.

Story #6: Uncle Bazvid (pronounced Baze-vid)

Around age 5, Dave and I were playing on a snow-hill in our back parking lot and some little girl in our housing project showed up and took a shine to my brother, whom she insisted on calling Uncle Baze-vid. He hated this, and

consequently this became my name for him for at least the next 10 years.

Story #7: Food - Part 1

I guess we didn't have a lot of money, as Mom was always buying canned vegetables on sale, or "fresh" stuff from the sale-bin. The result was that we ate a lot of canned lima beans, and other such delicacies. The one thing I couldn't handle in our culinary spectrum were brussel sprouts. For my parents to eat food, you had to cook the hell out of it, as in their world, food was filled with dangerous germs. The result was that our vegetables were tasteless mush, and if we had meat, it was like shoe-leather. Well, let me tell you, brussel sprouts were just about the worst thing in my world, and once every couple of months, Mom would find some dark-green brussel sprouts that had fallen under the vegetable trays and upon discovery, had been marked down to a price that even Mom couldn't resist, and put in the sale bin at our local grocery store: Steinbergs.[†] Coming home through the door from school, you could smell them on the stove, like a pot of bubbling sewage. It was like a death sentence, as there could be only one ending to the evening: me sitting alone at the table, pushing a smelly lump of cold brussel sprout around the plate, the mechanical kitchen timer slowly ticking down to zero, at which time I would be spanked and sent to bed. Yep - good times . . .

Aside from my bi-monthly brussel sprouts spanking (which somehow that little toad David appears to have managed to weasel his way out of?), the other bane of our young existence was powdered skim milk. This crap was somehow sold as food, despite its clearly toxic nature, and was irresistible to skinflints like my Mom. Our salvation

---

[†] I suspect Steinbergs is Hebrew for "epicurean wasteland"

was that even Dad couldn't handle powdered skim milk, and he would join us in rebelling against having to drink the stuff. Unfortunately, the old skinflint (aka Mom) couldn't bear to actually throw out the 50 lbs of skim milk formula that she somehow managed to embezzle from the Ethiopian Children's fund. The result was that this foul powder would keep making appearances in our real milk (as well as anything else that Mom cooked over the next decade that demanded some form of dairy product), and it was up to us to ferret out the presence of powdered skim-milk in our food, and then rat Mom out to Dad[†].

Maybe bad cooking and crappy food were Mom's ultimate revenge on us? Who knows?

[†] Interestingly, it was possible to detect powdered skim milk by looking at the meniscus on a glass: any taint of pale blue, and you knew that your drink had been poisoned.

3.1 Christmas

In the pre-Internet years, the number one place to figure out what you wanted for Christmas was the Sears Christmas catalog. The whole back part was kid stuff, and as soon as it showed up in September, my brother and I would go through it with fine-toothed comb, attempting to find exactly what had been missing from our souls - the one addition that would complete us. Once this was settled on, the bargaining, nagging, badgering, and whining would begin. Trying to not sound like I'm stealing this from Ralphie in "A Christmas Story," here is a typical conversation:

> **Paul:** "Hey Mom! I know what I want for Christmas. Let me show you."
>
> **Mom:** "Not now - I'm making supper. Later after supper."
>
> **Paul:** "It's a crane that has a control and can grab things. It's right here on Page 134. See?"
>
> **Mom:** *(unenthusiastically)* "Wow - that's nice. How much is it."
>
> **Paul:** "It's only $29.99!"
>
> **Mom:** "That's an awful lot of money!"
>
> **Paul:** "But I want it so much. Please, please, please . . ."

Anyway, you get the drift. This little charade would play out over the coming weeks, with us becoming more and more obsessed, and trying to work our Holy Grail of the Year into any conversation, and my parents putting up a stonewall of "It costs too much."

When Christmas approached, a present from my parents to me would inevitably appear under the tree that in no possible way could be construed as a model crane (or whatever the Holy Grail of that year was). I'd shake the box, get yelled at for trying to tunnel in past the wrapping without ripping anything, and perform a full shake-based analysis on the contents, with usually incorrect results. Seeing this obsessive behavior over the years, my parents rapidly realized that putting the actual present under the tree was useless, and so they started putting lovely decoy presents under the tree such as a roll of toilet paper in a box, with a note saying where the real goods lay. Ha, ha! Funny . . .

Anyway, we will return to Christmas later.

The Middle Years

In 1972, we moved back to our house from Edmonton, where my Dad had just completed (under duress) a 4 year computer science degree. His employer had given him the choice of going to Edmonton for 4 years to do his degree, and continue his career, or stay in Ottawa and never be promoted again[†]. He chose Edmonton, and we rented our house in Ottawa for 4 years to somebody who liked to paint. Every year in fact - in wonderful late 60's pastels, different in every room, over switch plates, all subsidized through the rental agreement with my Dad, who had agreed to pay for maintenance. This drove him mental, and the day we got back, he embarked on the restoration of the house back to its natural black and white state.

In the meantime, Dave and I had grown up, and grown more sophisticated.[‡] In this next section, I'll concentrate on food, as food, desserts, and meals provided hours of psychological fun.

[†] Apparently 2nd year calculus almost killed him and he had to beg for a passing grade, explaining his career situation to the prof and promising to "never darken your doorway again if you'll pass me". Years later, when I was in engineering, my Dad noticed that I had the same text book as him (Protter and Morrey), and ran down-stairs. After a few minutes of rummaging around in his old books, he came back upstairs and announced "It's those same two clowns!!" Sure enough, it was the exact same book. I promptly took mine back for a refund and switched to his. The first chapter was filled with precise, detailed notes. The second less so. By the third, the notes were gone . . .

[‡] And by sophisticated, I guess I mean that Dave started to fight back.

The "Letter Guy" and Other Stories

Story #8: Candies

In our house, we were typically not allowed more than one candy a day. Yet despite this snail's pace of consumption by Dave and I, there were always new, and varied licorice-based candies on top of the fridge. We never really connected the dots until years later, but what was basically happening was that our Dad was a closet licorice-candy fiend. In fact it should have been obvious. For instance, we'd go out on Hallowe'en trick-or-treating and come home with pillow-cases full of candy. Dad would then proceed to go through our haul to fish out any dangerous / suspicious items. Who would have known so many people liked to poison licorice? Dad also professed to "hate" chocolate, but regardless, never missed an opportunity to devour any chocolate that came within his reach. Consequently, lots of good chocolate was also extracted from our Hallowe'en loot by dear, caring Dad.

Dad also liked to bring us chocolate bars from the machines at his work. Well, it turned out that dear old Dad, in the process of buying chocolate bars for us, also happened to have one or two for himself - a fact I only got him to confess to recently.

Well - you can only stay in the closet so long, and one night I remember getting up to go to the bathroom, and I look down the hall and see the light on in the living room, and, lo and behold, Dad's sitting in an arm-chair reading - with the bowl of candy that should have been on top of the fridge - at his side. Worse - he was literally shovelling hand-fulls of the licorice candy into his mouth. I was dumbfounded!! This was my first experience with real, true hypocrisy, as NOBODY was supposed to be allowed more than one candy.

Story #9: Vegetables and Ice-Cream

In general, food became one of the focal points for our psychological warfare. David, for whatever reason, seemed to be squeamish about food, and was easily disgusted by a simple act like mixing vegetables into one's ice-cream. As a result, I felt compelled on a regular basis to save some vegetables from my lunch or dinner to mix into my dessert ice-cream, exclusively for Dave's viewing pleasure. Now the ice-cream we had was essentially crap (Ice Castle for those of you who remember it). If you dumped it into the sink, and let it melt, you'd get this nasty, gooey white mixture that seemed to have very little to do with cream. However, sweetened crap for dessert was better than no crap at all, so we dug into the Ice Castle with relish. Mom typically didn't eat dessert, and if Dad did, he'd wolf it down, so after lunch (or dinner) there'd usually just be Dave and I at the table. And out would come the vegetables. Just mixing a few peas into a spoonful of ice-cream was enough to send Dave into convulsions. He'd literally gag and retch, cursing me out as a soulless son of Satan. I'd agree, load up some more vegetables into my ice-cream and deliver another psychological blow to him. Of course the vegetables in my ice-cream tasted horrible, but it was all worth it.

Story #10: Half

Something I learned long ago from David, was that if I got something, he got either half, or a duplicate. Well, one day a brilliant thought struck me: "I'll wait for David to want something, and then I'll demand my half!." Here's how it went down. Mom had made some Betty Crocker vanilla cake, and there was one piece left. I was sitting in the living room, and Dave wanders in the back door. He sees the cake and then proceeds to ask Mom if he can have it. At that very instant I spring into action, and demand my half of the cake too.

Since we couldn't be trusted with even a simple act like cutting a piece of cake in half, Mom had to come and cut it in half for us. Dave was pissed, as he'd figured he was going to get the whole piece of cake. Wrongo! But hold onto your seat, dear reader, as the really genius part is about to come!

As soon as Ma had left the room, I took my plate to the garbage can, and, making sure that Dave was watching, scraped my half of the cake into the garbage. Dave looked ready to have a heart-attack!

"Mom! Paul just threw his piece of cake into the garbage!" wailed David.

Mom came storming upstairs, not even waiting for a commercial, demanding to know what the hell my problem was.

"It's my half, and I can do what I want with it." I explained somewhat lamely.

Needless to say, I had just signed myself up for another spanking when Dad got home. But - as every good prankster knows - it was worth it, just to see Dave turn red with disbelief and rage. Yep - good times . . .

Story #11: Standard Table Pranks

As pretty much any boy knows, there are all sorts of "humourous" things that can be done to condiments and things of this nature. There's the tried and true "Salt in the sugar bowl trick," as well as the standard loosening of the tops of things like salt shakers, soy-sauce bottles, etc. All of these lead to predictable, but not terribly satisfying outcomes. However the trick is to make sure that only the intended recipient receives the doctored container - or there will spankings all around. Of course all of these

things were done to each other by us, but none of them were very rewarding, as it was all rather pedestrian.

However, there were a couple of stunts that were developed in our little crucible that are noteworthy. One is (to my knowledge) unique to Canada, and involved the use of the quart plastic bags that low-cost milk in Canada came in. These plastic bags that were shaped like little rectangular pillows, and then you placed this bag in a pitcher (that was designed for the bag), and then cut the end of the bag, allowing it to be poured. Now, I'm sure that

Figure 4.1 **Milk bag in pitcher**

you the reader, are thinking, "Wow - this would be fun to throw at cars on a highway," or some such stunt as this, but no - the real genius with a bag of milk, was to wait until the

milk got down about half-way, and then make a second cut in the bag just at the lip of the pitcher. Then, the unsuspecting dupe who was pouring himself (or God-forbid! - herself!) some milk would instead pour the milk in front of the glass or bowl. It was priceless!

Story #12: Nuts

Now up until this point, I have only told you about things that I primarily did to my brother, or others, but these next two are Dave's, and I have to take my hat off to him on these. The first one involves Christmas nuts. Every year, our parents would buy a bag of mixed nuts and put them out in a bowl. Our Dad loved nothing better (after licorice and chocolate) than to spend a peaceful Sunday afternoon devouring nuts. Well, one day Dave gets this genius idea to crack open the walnuts along the seam, dig the nut meat out, fill the nut shells back up with saw-dust, and then glue the halves back together. Then he'd take the doctored nuts and put them back in the bowl. Well, just imagine your horror at happily cracking open nuts, and then getting one from which this stream of sawdust pours out. It's like you're holding the black plague in your hands, and your mind immediately leaps to thoughts about what sort of nasty thing could do this to a nut! Many a visitor to our house fell victim to this little prank, with always the same result! Priceless!

Story #13: Coke Bottles

The second genius idea that my brother got was to doctor the remnants of some drink in the fridge. For instance, Mom would periodically make some sort of Kool-Aid, or buy some generic cola drink, and when you came in from playing outside, you'd be thirsty and want to take a big gulp of whatever was in the fridge. Seeing just enough of something to drink in the fridge made it even sweeter, as you could cheat your brother out of getting the last of it,

and you didn't have to resort of tap water (which frankly was pretty good in Ottawa).

Well, one day I come in from screwing around outside, and I see that there's a couple of mouthfuls of generic cola left in the fridge. So, I grab the bottle, tip it back, and just about puke. Dave had replaced the coke with a mixture of vinegar, water, and soy-sauce. Nice![†]

Story #14: Fake Milk

At one point in the 70's there was a Joke Shop in Ottawa that serviced the pre-teen market for whoopee cushions, fake puke, and the like. Needless to say, it was a favorite place of ours, but unfortunately this stuff cost money - a lot of money, so we never actually bought anything. We just went with our friends, let them buy the stuff, and then borrowed it. One of the very convincing items that we borrowed was a glass of fake spilled milk. What this was, was a glass tipped over on its side, with the milk all spilt out. Only the milk was actually a soft plastic that looked identical to milk, and was attached to the glass.

One weekend, Dave and I found ourselves in possession of this "fake milk" and so we decided to try it out on Mom. Now, as I have stressed numerous times already, this was a dicey proposition at best, as Mom usually found nothing that we did funny. However, it was a boring day, and we figured we'd give things a go. So, we positioned the fake milk on the living room floor between the carpets and headed off downstairs for some television[‡].

About 2 hours later (in fact we'd by then forgotten about the milk!) Mom comes storming down the stairs and starts

---

[†] In writing this, I realize now that my brother probably is a closet poisoner.

cursing us out for being worthless, lazy bastards who'd just leave a glass of milk lying on the floor, and not clean it up and expecting her to do it. Immediately remembering, we went up with her to "clean it up." I walked over, picked it up, and held it out for Mom to see that it was fake. It made no difference! She was still just as mad as if it had been the real thing! In her eyes, it was if we had done it, and the fact that it was a joke didn't detract from her belief that we probably would have just left real milk lying on the floor, expecting that she "our slave" would just deal with it. Unbelievable!

---

‡ Now I have to go off on a monologue here, as for whatever reason, in the 60's and 70's everybody wanted to cover up their hardwood floors with crazy colored carpet (and OK - prior to urethane, having to wax and strip the floors was probably good enough reason). Our house was no exception, and we went with olive green carpet. However we didn't go wall-to-wall, but area / path. What this meant was that we left a strip of about 8" around the outer edge of the carpet, and made little paths with the carpet down the hall and to the front door. The whole concept is bizarre, but it's what my parents came up with as the perfect compliment to the gold drapes, egg-shell white walls, and red paisley chairs (see the picture of Cat in Figure 2.1). Incidentally, these chairs were later replaced with brown Naughahyde futon-style couches with a green / gold tartan weave on the seats. Very classy!

4.1 Other Activities

Story #15: The Crooked Kitchen

One summer day, I was particularly bored, so I decided to start experimenting with what our kitchen would look like tilted by 10°. To accomplish this, I set about propping up all of the kitchen chairs and table, so that they were canted to the right by 10°. It looked pretty cool, so I decided to finish the scene off by canting the clock, pictures, crap on the counter, etc. I even tied off Mom's hanging plant with fishing line so that is was canted at 10° as well. When I was done it looked pretty impressive. Especially when viewed from the back door - which is the door through which everybody entered and exited the house from. Satisfied with my work, I then lay down on the coach in the living room to read a book.

About a hour later, I hear this shriek from the back door followed by a "Paul! You Mutt!!." Mom had come home. Interested to see what was what, I walked out of the living room, and found her clutching onto the railing by the back door, eyes tightly shut. Well, it turns out that Ma had the worst sort of inner ear affliction. The kind that is so bad, that you don't even need any actual motion: just thinking about a boat tossing and turning in a storm is enough to make you sea-sick. Well it turns out that tipping the horizon by 10° was enough to send Mom reeling. Who knew?

Story #16: Baby-sitting Dave

One day, my parents were foolish enough to leave Dave and some dopey friend of his alone in my care. My best friend Sandy was also around (there is an entire section devoted to him in Section 4.6), and we had just seen Conan The Barbarian at the theatre, and were particularly struck by how much our clothesline in the backyard resembled the grist-mill device that the slaves were tied to

at the beginning of the Conan movie. You see, while all the houses initially had these breeches-buoy type of clothes lines that consisted of a one pulley on the side of the house, and another on the telephone pole across the yard, we went upscale and installed this thing that looked like a square antenna mounted on a rotating pole. The "antenna" was in reality a bunch of clothes lines, and you could rotate it so that the wind hit the clothes just right.

Well, let me tell you, it didn't take long for us to realize that we had our own grist mill, and a couple of slaves that needed to turn it. So, my friend and I tied my brother and his friend to the clothesline, got some lawn-chairs and the garden hose (to motivate them to walk), and sat down to watch them walk in a circle. It felt pretty good, until my parents came home, and I got in trouble.[†]

[†] Surprisingly not that much trouble. Either my parents thought it was pretty hilarious, or they were just getting used to us, but regardless, not much happened to me for this!

4.2 The Bathroom

This area deserves it's own section because of the many deep, and varied stunts that occurred here.

Story #17: Showers

There are few pranks that satisfy so much, or are as cruel as, a good cold-water shower incident. It is unclear who started it, or whether it was just an accident caused by flushing the toilet in our house while somebody was in the shower. Like all houses built in Canada in the late 1950's, early 1960's, plumbing consisted of a single 1/2" pipe that snaked its way from the hot-water tank at one end of the house, past every sink and toilet, and finally dead-ended at the shower in the lone bathroom at the other end of the house. Naturally, any turning on of hot-water at a sink, or flushing a toilet, would significantly alter the temperature, and as a result, the enjoyment level of a nice, hot shower. It was almost as bad as if you physically went down to the shut-off valve on the hot-water tank and just plain turned it off - usually around the time the victim had soaped up their face. Naturally, this became de rigeur for a decade-long war in which Dave, my Dad, and I tortured each other in the shower. If it wasn't the hot-water tank, the other standard thing to do was fill up a bucket with cold water, and dump it over the shower curtain. My douche-bag brother Dave honed this idea even further by adding a bunch of ice-cubes into the bucket for the "piece de la resistance," of which I was the first recipient.

Basically, none of us had a peaceful shower in over a decade. There were continuously shifting alliances and fragile truces, which inevitably broke down. Worse, our single bathroom had the standard bathroom "lock" that could be easily defeated by any 5-year old with a pen refill or coat-hanger. Despite that, you'd still lock the door before attempting to shower. I remember vividly waiting until

people had gone to bed, or were downstairs watching TV, and then sneaking into the bathroom to have a shower. You'd lock the door, jump in quietly, and then frantically soap up one part of your body, pausing every few seconds to check to make sure nobody was creeping into the bathroom with a bucket of water. Then you'd test the shower water temperature, rinse off, and then try cleaning another part of your body. Then just when you thought you were out of the woods: SPLASH! Over the curtain would come a bucket of ice-water. Or, the hot water would vanish, or sometimes all of the water would be shut off.

Incredibly, the worst instigator of this war was not Dave or I, but Dad. Consequently, this story has an interesting foot-note, in that after I moved out of the house, I came back one chilly spring morning in time for my Dad's shower. He ran his morning schedule like a railroad, with him entering the shower at precisely 7:00am. Consequently, showing up in time to ambush him didn't take much planning. So, at precisely 7:01am I dragged the garden hose with the sprayer attachment on the end through the back door of the house, walked in the bathroom door, threw open the shower curtain, and hosed him down with ice-cold water. And to this day, I have never been paid back for that one. It felt good[†] . . .

Story #18: Soap and Toothbrushes

One time my Dad's uncle came and stayed with us for a week. He was kind of wacked, and had long, white hair that he liked to pile up in a sort of ice-cream cone fashion on his head. He had round, coke-bottle lens glasses and looked vaguely like the crazy uncle on the Flintstones. He was also not the paragon of bathroom cleanliness, and I remember Dave and I talking about how disgusted we

---

[†] I think I even said "Up against the wall white-man!"

were, having to pull his long white hairs off the shower soap. Dave - the dick genius that he was, promptly joined the dots, and set up a surprise for me.

A few weeks after our dear uncle left, I go into the shower, and grab the soap. To my disgust, I find a wad of hair, and a couple of Dave's toenails sticking out of the soap. I came very close to puking.

My revenge, while maybe not sounding that bad, was to wedge a bunch of green hot-dog relish into Dave's toothbrush, which lead to the desired result of Dave rolling around on the bathroom floor, retching. I guess it looked pretty bad, as to this day, he still seems to be traumatized by relish.

Story #19: The Toilet

Every once in a while, you'd come home from school and want to have a crap. You'd go into the bathroom, lock the door, sit down, and start your business. I don't know who started it,[†] but the toilet was a long way from the door, so if you were in the middle of things, and the door opened, there was nothing you could do about it. Well, one day, one of us decided to open the door while the other was having a crap, and just leave it open for Mom to find. This then rapidly evolved into one of us opening the door, and proclaiming:

"Ugh! Dave - you sick pig! Close the door!," followed by

"Mom! Dave's crapping without shutting the door again!"

Later on, I improved on things in the bathroom with the acquisition of some fire-crackers a friend of mine procured

---

[†] I believe this was Dave's stunt

for me in South Carolina. You see, back in the 60's Canada was a fun place, where you could buy firecrackers and blow up your old Hot-Wheels, as God intended for them to be blown up. However, I guess it was all fun "until somebody lost an eye" and that was the end of fire-crackers in Canada. Fortunately, many people I knew routinely went vacationing in Florida, and to get to Florida from Ottawa you went through the land of unregulated fun - South Carolina. Now, to this day I have never been there, but as a kid, it sounded like the promised land of explosives.

Anyway, as soon as somebody I knew headed down there, I gave them $20 of my hard-earned allowance money that was saved for just such an event as this, and instructed them to bring back all the fire-crackers my money could buy.

Well - as soon as I got my hands on the firecrackers, I set about experimenting with them. One of the things I found was that the fuzing on them was quite predicable, and that if you lit one, you knew basically when to throw it so it would explode in the air. Similarly, if you taped it to a piece of card-board (so it wouldn't wreck Mom's floor upon detonation), you could stick it under the bathroom door at precisely the moment it was going to explode!

Let me tell you, it was one hell of a bang in the small bathroom, followed by a whoosh of air out from under the door. About once a month, I felt compelled to give my brother the "firecracker-under-the-bathroom-door" treatment. It helped make him the man he is today. I still remember him moaning on the toilet about his ears afterwards. Ah - good times!

Story #20: The Sink Sprayer

I almost forgot about this one! My sick douchebag-of-a-brother Dave invented this, and I have to take my hat off to him on this, as it is genius in both it's simplicity and devastating effect. Basically, he took an elastic band and tied it around the sink sprayer in our kitchen sink so that the diverter lever was always pressed. Then he aimed the sink sprayer at where the hapless victim (aka the poor bastard who happened to turn on the sink) would be standing and waited for the expected shriek. It worked so well that it became a standard stunt, and you basically had to check if the sprayer had been booby-trapped every time you turned on the sink. Many times it was, and you'd smile that inner smile that comes from outsmarting your enemy, but every once in a while - you'd forget to check and "Blam!" A blast of cold water to the chest! Good times . . .

As a footnote to this story, my Dad figured out that if you held the sprayer against the screen window in front of the kitchen sink, it would shoot through the screen as if it weren't there. The result was that nobody could walk past the kitchen window without getting spritzed.

4.3 Cat

We got Cat sometime in the early 1970's. Mom wanted one, probably for companionship, given the lack of anything coming from our childish, self-absorbed direction. She was a black Siamese variant that we got as a kitten from some farming friend Dad knew. Once in our place, she was rapidly integrated into our fun.

Story #21: Attacking David

Now cats are basically very lazy, but deep within their cat souls is a crazed desire for action, that emerges every so often. When they don't want to play, they are masters at ignoring you. You can pile a string on their face, roll marbles past them, put tea-towels over their back - nothing. It is as if they were a million miles away. However, if you can get them going, and pry open that crazed part of their soul, then they are lots of acrobatic fun.

Every night after dinner one of us (Dad, Dave, or I) would put on a leather glove, get a paper shopping bag with a hole in the end, and some string and run Cat around. She particularly loved to dive into the bag, and then fish things (such as string or fingers or dry cat-food) into the bag via the hole. Nothing tasted better than some cat-food that she fished through a hole. She even got so that she'd tear her own hole in the corner of new shopping bags in anticipation of fun.

Anyway, one time during these events, she found that she could "attack" Dave and chase him down the hall. I guess she sensed the weak link in the chain and went right after it. What she'd do in the morning or evening, was hide on a chair under the kitchen table, and wait for a barefoot Dave to go by. Then as soon as he passed by, she'd dive at his feet, putting her paws around his ankle, and give him a few

nips[†] sending Dave running, with her chasing behind. It was hilarious - Dave terrorized by the cat!

Story #22: Hide and Go Seek

Now Dave wasn't going to let this just go by, so he (and I) would try and sneak up on Cat and scare her. It was basically hopeless, as cats have crazy sharp senses. To illustrate this point, we'd play hide-and-go seek with Cat. One of us would go and hide, while the other kept Cat from seeing where the other would go. Then we'd let her loose, and she'd just wander to whatever hiding place the other was in, regardless of where in the house he went, and sit outside. Only by ambushing her in full flight could you get any satisfaction. For instance, one of us would put a blanket over our shoulders so you could spread it out like bat wings, and then go and roust a sleeping Cat, making threatening growling sounds and flapping the blanket. She'd immediately tear off down the stairs to head up into the basement ceiling, where on the way one of us would jump out a room at the bottom of the stairs, and try to tickle her on the way by.

Story #23: Cat Psychology

While it was fun at first chasing Cat, she'd periodically just ignore you regardless of how "scary" things were, and a lot of the time you got the feeling that she was just playing along, even expecting an ambush. As a result, we'd start doing other things.

One thing we discovered was that Cat hated to be watched when she was having a piss or a crap. Consequently, whenever we got the chance (which wasn't very often), we'd see her wander off into her room (which doubled as

---

[†] It's not like she was some kind of trained attack cat: this was real playing with no blood.

the furnace room) and then go and hang around her, ruining her peace and quiet. She'd sit there, avoiding eye contact, with her ears half back, finishing her business while you enjoyed her catly discomfort.

Another thing we'd do is build a wall of couch-pillows in the basement with one little hole guarded by a hand in a leather glove, and try and keep her in her half, while we hung out on the other side. She'd play along making sort of half-assed attempts to climb the wall, which was designed to fall inwards, or try to "nice" her way past the glove, but we were having none of it. Finally she'd hear Mom opening some can of tuna in the kitchen, or just get bored and she'd just jump over the wall. She could easily clear 6'.

Story #24: The Area Rug

One of the rules that Cat had to abide by was not going into the living room or bedrooms, but she figured that if she stuck to the hardwood edging of the living room floor, she'd be OK. We eventually cracked on this and let her get away with it. However, she was never allowed to climb on the beds or the furniture. Despite this, her favorite place to sleep was on one of the stupid tartan couches in the living room. You'd come home and find a lazy Cat slowly walking through the kitchen happily greeting you as if there was nothing wrong, but if you went into the living room, you'd find a warm spot on the couch where she'd been sleeping. A lot of times when you were heading off in the car, you'd see her face at the front window watching you leave. But if you ran back in to catch her, she'd be lazily walking around the kitchen, with no idea of what anybody was excited about.

Story #25: The Squirrels

Cat liked to spend most of her time outside, and maybe because of our nightly wrestling with her, she was a good fighter, and despite numerous scraps never came away with any serious injury or loss of ear. One particular thorn in her side was this calico cat named Fluff that lived two houses away. They basically hated each other, and would fight a lot.[†] However, the one thing that they hated more than each other were the neighborhood squirrels, so if a squirrel showed up, they'd cooperate to try and catch it. All of this was basically hopeless, as a squirrel can do acrobatic jumps that cats can only dream of. For instance, if Cat and Fluff were fighting and a squirrel showed up, they'd immediately chase the squirrel up the closest tree. Cat, being the better climber, would tear up the tree after it while Fluff guarded the bottom. However the squirrel would just run off to the upper part of the tree, while Cat labored after it. Then once Cat got close, the squirrel would just make some amazing leap to a neighboring tree leaving the two cats looking foolish.

Along the back of our yard was a fence that both squirrels and neighborhood cats would walk along.[‡] One spring day, after the new batch of baby squirrels were out playing, Fluff and Shadow (aka Cat) showed up and managed to trap a baby squirrel between them on the fence, while Mom squirrel sat on the fence on the other side of Shadow. Finally it looked like the cats were going to score some squirrel. The baby grew frantic, and ran back and forth

---

[†] And by fighting, I mean the standard cat chess game of staring each other to death over a couple-of-hours period from different positions interspersed by about 5 seconds of actual action.

[‡] On the other side of the fence was a terrier that just couldn't quite reach the top of the fence, so consequently both cats and squirrels would hang out there while the terrier below went mental.

between the two cats a couple of times, turning back at the last second, as Mom squirrel looked like she was getting ready to attack Shadow. Finally the baby squirrel just charged straight at Shadow. Shadow reared up into the classic cat defense position, back arched, ears back flat, fur fluffed, and mouth open in a full hiss, while the baby squirrel ran straight between Shadow's legs to Mom. Shadow deflated with a stunned look. It was hilarious.

4.4 Christmas

Christmas - once we got past the Sears catalog and fake presents, was now driven by us as teenagers.

Story #26: The Christmas Tree

Putting up the Christmas tree inevitably fell to my Mom, who as we got older placed more and more of the task on us. We had a fake tree consisting of a shaft with holes in it, and an array of branches that fit in the holes, ranging in size from small to large. For a couple of years we put it together properly, until one year I realized that there was no strict requirement to make it conical with the point at the top. So one year we put it together as an inverted cone. My mother was not impressed, and after some lame arguments about how creative we were, we had to disassemble the whole thing and put it together properly. A lot of work, for unappreciated art.

Next year we took a short-cut to art, and essentially put the tree together properly, but had two large branches sticking out the top to look like moose antlers. Again, Mom was unimpressed, but seemed to see a little humor in it this time.

Story #27: The Mop and Bucket

One year I got the genius idea of wrapping up a mop and bucket as gifts to my Mom. I purchased them and then proceeded to wrap them in newspaper so that it was obvious what they were (wasting that much real wrapping paper would not have been deemed "funny"). You think I would have learned from the fake spilled milk, but no - I had to go and poke the sleeping bear. Mom was not impressed, and instead of the mirth and gaiety that my subtle jest was supposed to engender in her, I found myself being yelled at for being an insensitive jerk.

Story #28: Tinsel Kitty

Once again, Cat reappears in the rich tapestry of this book. She had some obsession with climbing trees, and while good at going up, sucked at going down. The Christmas tree was no different. While in the living room and technically out of bounds, she routinely climbed up the interior of the thing, causing all sorts of shaking and dropping of ornaments.

She also developed an unnatural love of tinsel, which wound up hanging out her butt throughout the Yuletide. She cleaned herself well, so it wasn't a sanitary hazard, but it tended to be disconcerting for guests to see our cat bedecked in this silvery holiday "garb."

4.5 External Stupidity

I was a major pyromaniac. Nothing gave me more joy than making explosives or pyrotechnics. Unfortunately, as I sadly discovered in 1st year chemistry, what I actually enjoyed was not chemistry, but alchemy. Nevertheless, I spent many a good year building my pyrotechnical knowledge, as well as my collection of chemicals.

My lab was in the laundry room in the basement, which was directly underneath the kitchen. After school, I'd head downstairs for experiments that I'd planned from the evening before. I used to synchronize my experiments with my Mom's cooking, so that when I tested some new pyrotechnic, it coincided with dinner. A little extra smoke, with a bit of a potassium perchlorate / sulphur smell to it? Hey - dinner was ready. I kid you not - I went on for years like this. You see, in the early 70's my parents had a religious experience and became born-again Christians. So instead of hanging out with their kids, and seeing what they were up to, they (primarily my Dad) were busy reading the Bible. Fine by me, let me tell you, as it gave me free reign to try all sorts of cool things. One of the coolest was nitrogen triiodide.

Story #29: Nitrogen Triiodide

Back in the day, when people weren't so concerned about Al Qaeda and the like, you could pretty much walk into any drug store and buy all sorts of dubious chemicals. For instance potassium nitrate was an over-the-counter purchase. God knows what it was legitimately used for, but there it was: stocked as a standard item in Canadian drug stores, just waiting to be turned into gun-powder. But the Grand-Daddy of all drug stores was Habermann Chemists on 192 Laurier West.[†] This place was the motherload of chemicals. You could literally walk into this place, and if you had your story straight about what you were going to

do with a chemical - they'd sell it to you. You couldn't buy beer or cigarettes, but you could buy as much potassium perchlorate as you wanted. Same with things like metallic iodine, sodium, potassium - you name it, it was there for the taking, and age be damned. All you needed was a story. You can't imagine how many "oxygen-generation for astronauts" experiments I ran as a 13 year old.

Fueling my creativity, was the presence in our high-school library of some "Fun With Science" experiment books from the 1940's and 1950's. Apparently, back then, it was good old family fun to build your own arc-welder out of carbon rods from a D-cell battery, lead sinkers, and a pyrex dish full of salt-water. I remember firing that baby up with a dubious Dad who had to help me attach the lead sinkers to bare wires from an old lamp cord. Even I was scared when that thing went off - the wires started melting, the water in the dish was boiling like hell, and then the fuse blew. But at least we got an arc going for about 15 seconds!

Aside from other lawsuit generating experiments, the book contained the formula for a substance called nitrogen triiodide. Now this stuff was unstable as hell, having some extra electron hanging around that only the presence of water somehow mitigated.[†] Whatever - it blew up, I had the formula, and I had the materials (or would shortly). After some library work to concoct a reason why a teenager needed potassium iodide, metallic iodine, and ammonium hydroxide, I headed off to Habermann's to pick up the goods. Unfortunately, the metallic iodine was crazy expensive, and knowing that our chemistry lab at school

---

[†] The fact that 30+ years later I still remember the address of this probably long-vanished establishment speaks volumes.

[†] If you want to actually know about this stuff, take it to the web, as I am writing this from my head, and since the point of this story is the story, and not the substance . . . well you figure it out.

had some of the stuff, I decided to hold off on buying it until I knew it was worthwhile.

Next day, I asked our science teacher if I could create a little experiment over lunch.[†] No problem. I followed the old "Fun With Science" recipe and cranked out this purplish mush on filter papers. Poking it did nothing, so I distributed it around the school's green-house to dry, and headed off to afternoon classes.

After classes, I rushed back to the chemistry lab, to find a really pissed off teacher. Apparently, I didn't clean up so good, and as things started to dry, the action started. Some girl turned on a tap, the water hit the sink, and "Bam!" an explosion. Someone else picked up a Florence flask, and "Bam!" it explodes and they drop it. Then, there were loud explosions throughout the afternoon coming from the greenhouse. All this was music to my ears! The secrets of the ancients unlocked! I rushed into the greenhouse, and looked at my collection of papers with the purplish mush. Most of them were now empty and ripped up, but a few still had some dried mush on them. Cautiously, I grabbed a broom and jabbed a paper with the handle. Snap! I poked another paper. Nothing. I poked a third, which had a large pile of mush on it, and "Wham!" It was like a stun grenade: my vision caved in from the edges in a brownish wave, and I was left staggering around. Wow! Metallic iodine was worth every cent!!!

I promptly headed back to Habermann's and forked over the money.

[†] They had much better equipment then my basement lab, and this way I could keep an eye on things without Mom wandering into the laundry room.

You know though, despite having this perfect prank formula in my possession, I wasn't able to do anything with it, as the school had heard about my lab work. However my brother was able to put it to good use!

A couple of years later, David wanted revenge on some teacher of his, so I cranked out another batch of the stuff for him, and he (or one of his friends) loaded up the classroom door-knob with the stuff. Apparently, it worked like a charm, and despite the best efforts of the school's science department, nobody was able to figure out what happened. A really cool side effect of the explosion turned out to be iodine staining, which was vividly seen on the teacher's hand. Fun!

Story #30: The End of the Lab

The end of my pyrotechnical career occurred one winter night when I was hand grinding some gunpowder with a mortar and pestle. My parents and brother were in bed, and I hit something in the mixture that sparked and the whole affair went up, burning the back of my hand. I washed it off, but with a sickening feeling, realized that all of my skin on the back of my hand was sloughing off, and this was beyond my ability to deal with. I was forced to go upstairs and face the music. Mom was pissed at having to get up, so Dad took me over to the emergency room, where the doctor proceeded to ask what I was doing. Dad was half asleep in the hospital waiting room, as the doctor quizzed me on what I was up to.

"Grinding some charcoal" I replied.

"Hmmm - that shouldn't ignite like that. What else was in there?" he continued.

"Umm - maybe some sulphur?," I said, starting to notice my Dad beginning to pay attention.

"Hmmm - still that shouldn't burn like that. Are you sure there wasn't anything else in there?" he queried.

"Uh - maybe a little potassium nitrate?" I stammered. I saw Dad starting to put together what was what, and he even asked "Isn't potassium nitrate saltpeter[†]?" I looked pleadingly at the doctor, and God bless him, he saw what was happening and let it go, changing the subject. Nevertheless this little incident led to my parents calling the fire-marshall to see what I had going on in the laundry room. He was horrified, and told my parents that if there was a fire, their insurance would be void, and that was the end.

There is a somewhat ironic postscript to this story. Several years later, one warm Sunday afternoon, I was at home, with nothing to do so I decided to burn some "evil" fungus out of the garden shed with methyl hydrate - which is basically fondue fuel. There was a plastic jug of the stuff still in the basement, and I also had a large syringe left from my lab, so I got a lighter and proceeded to "flamethrower" the fungus into oblivion. Unfortunately, you can barely see a methyl hydrate flame in full sunlight, so I was unable to notice if the tip of my syringe was burning. After a few flame-throwerings, I put the syringe back into the methyl hydrate and the fumes in the bottle ignited, burning all of the skin off the back of my same hand! Ma was pissed! I think her words were "You idiot!," and she said that if I wanted to go to the hospital (which was about 10 minutes from our house) I'd have to do it myself, as she was making dinner. So, I wrapped my hand in a rag, got on my bike, and did it all over again. I haven't made any pyrotechnics since, and the damned fungus survived.

[†] Probably from being educated by that old Star-Trek episode where Kirk makes a diamond cannon.

Story #31: Fire On Deck

One day at my parents house, I decided to have some friends over for a barbecque. As my Mom was averse to fire (I wonder why . . .), instead of using normal lighter fluid to ignite their charcoal briquettes, my parents had this plug-in electric starter that looked like a handball racket frame made of stove-element material. I personally disliked it, but it eventually worked.

I made a heap of charcoal around this starter and plugged it in. Fifteen minutes later I returned to check on the progress and nothing. Lifting out the starter, an inch-long piece of the heating element fell off, and I was on to plan "B" - my old friend methyl hydrate, which still lived in the basement. I liberally dosed the charcoal pile and lit it on fire. To my utter astonishment, the ignition point of the charcoal appeared to be just on the edge of the methyl hydrate flame temperature, and after the methyl hydrate had burned off, only a few small edges of the charcoal were turning white. On to plan "C" - the blow dryer. I figured if I had some edges burning, and hit it with some forced air, I could get it to take off. Unfortunately, I forgot about the ashes from numerous other barbecques, and instead of accelerating the ignition of the briquettes that were starting to burn, the whole thing turned into this ash tornado. I was covered in ash, the deck was covered in ash, and the briquettes were out, and I was pissed.

OK - time for the "sure thing": gasoline. I blew off the deck with the blow dryer, pulled the briquette pile apart to make sure nothing was burning and then got about half a cup of gasoline in a can. Still unsure about whether the charcoal briquettes were entirely extinguished, and with the previous hand-burn incidents in my brain, I tossed the gas into the briquette pile from about 2 feet away. Wham! The whole thing went up in towering inferno, along with a bunch

of gas that missed the barbecque entirely and landed on the deck.

My brother's bedroom looked onto the deck, and when he was inside showing some friend of his something, he looked up to see orange flames outside his window. He and his friend immediately came running out, in time to see me wrestling with the garden hose, trying to turn it on. His idiot friend collapsed on the ground laughing while I finally extinguished the fire and gave up on supper.

The end of the story was that I wound up having to sand the burn marks and re-paint the deck, and from then on always started briquettes with gasoline cold, and never as plan "B."

4.6 My Friend Sandy

One of the players who drifted in and out of our activities was my friend Sandy. He lived in an essentially lawless family with two younger brothers. The first time I was at their place, we played cops and robbers with sawed off air-rifles, firing soggy catfood at each other. It hurt, but was pretty cool. Whereas my house had nothing really fun except my chemistry lab, Sandy's house was full of small engines, sawed-off air-rifles, sling-shots, and other such stuff. Together we had a paper route that consisted of two apartment buildings and a new residential neighborhood.

Story #32: The Paper Route

At the time, there were two competing papers in Ottawa: The Citizen, and The Journal. Naturally all of the paper-boys for these papers were at war with each other, as if you could piss off a customer who was with the competition and get them to switch to you, there was more money in it for you. We were with the Citizen and there were two of us, and only one carrier on the Journal route. Now you couldn't do anything really bad to the competing paper-boys, but dirty tricks were certainly allowed. First off there was the race from school to get to the papers first, as whoever got to the drop-off first usually cut the binding on the other guy's papers, so the wind would blow them away. Then there was random spitting in the competition's papers: you wouldn't do them all, but only certain vulnerable customers whom you figure you could wear down enough to get to switch.

The cleverest thing we did involved collection. Since the bulk of our customers lived in an apartment building, we figured there'd be a lot of single people, trying to work dates on the weekend. Consequently, what we'd do is track accounts until somebody owed us just more than $5. Then we'd get a bunch of coins and go collecting around

9:00pm on Friday night, right during prime romance time. Here's the scene: You are having a great date, and just as things are getting really hot, the door-bell starts to ring. You ignore it, but it rings again, and again. Finally you throw a house-coat on and open the door, ready to yell at whoever's there. Unfortunately, it's the two douche-bag teenagers who deliver your paper, whom you know you haven't paid in several weeks. So you run back to get your wallet and hand over $10. Finally after waiting for several minutes while the two idiots fumble through a pile of quarters to make your change, you finally say - "Forget it - just go, and give me credit for the extra." Nobody ever remembered what they gave us, and we could usually rake in an extra $3 - $4 per customer this way. It was genius!

Story #33: The Go-Cart

After about a year together, we decided to build a go-cart. Sandy managed to get the steering mechanism and wheels, and then we lashed a 10 hp Briggs & Stratton snow-blower engine onto it for power, and we were in business. The thing was totally dangerous, and would do around 50 mph on city streets. The brake was a belt nailed to a lever, which slowed down a pulley on the back left wheel. Cops stopped us routinely, but we told them it was an experimental vehicle, because we had heard somewhere (probably from some reliable source like one of our other school buddies) that it was OK to drive without a license if the vehicle was "experimental."

Story #34: The Snowmobile

After a year of harassment by the police, we traded the go-cart for an old snowmobile. This beast had a big single-cylinder, two-stroke, Sachs engine, and miraculously it worked. Consequently we were able to use it to deliver papers whenever the roads were impassable in the winter-time. Fortunately (in our opinion), the roads

were impassable almost all the time, and as a result we "had" to use the snowmobile. The coolest part about the neighborhood in our paper-route was that it was new. Consequently there was no real landscaping in place, so you could drive the snow-mobile at 60 mph across the front-yards of the development. Which is precisely what we'd do: terrorize the Journal carrier, deliver the papers, work on a few new converts, sell any extra papers to the convenience store at the end of the street, and then head to the new McDonald's by the Science and Tech Museum at 60 mph on the snow-mobile, bouncing over the lawns and driveways.

Unfortunately, this all came to an end one rainy winter night, when we tried to get the snowmobile running. It was covered in ice, and we couldn't get the key in, so we hosed some lock deicer on (basically methyl hydrate). Unfortunately this took far longer to melt ice than we had patience for, so we then got the bright idea of melting the ice with a propane torch. Duh! Immediately the lock deicer caught on fire, and burned the cowling of the snowmobile as well as the wiring-harness to the ground. It never ran again.

Story #35: Moving

A minor piece of foolishness to note about Sandy and I, was that at one point some guy in one of our apartments was moving from the 11th floor to the 4th floor, and he asked us to help him for $25. Being 15, this sort of money was gold, so we immediately agreed. At the end of the move, all we had to do was check the old apartment, and get rid of an arm-chair that he didn't want anymore. I guess we were supposed to take it downstairs to the dumpster in the basement, but we figured we'd try to jam it into the garbage chute first. Obviously, it didn't fit. Then it hit us! Why not heave it over the balcony? I mean - who hasn't

wondered what would happen to an arm-chair after an eleven story fall? Fortunately, under the guy's balcony there were only some bushes, so over the railing the chair went. It fell surrealistically slow, getting smaller and smaller until it crashed into the bushes. We raced downstairs to inspect our handiwork, but it took us a while to even find the chair, as it was compacted into a 6" tall pile of cloth and wood splinters. BUT - at least we now had scientific proof about the surviveability of an arm-chair after a high-speed impact!

As a short foot-note to this story, we headed back upstairs to see if there was anything else we could test. I mean, how often do you have access to an 11th floor balcony? Fortunately, the guy had left about 6 eggs in his fridge, which we promptly threw at cars on the road. Not terribly satisfying after the chair, but still interesting - especially in learning how to compensate for the drop when throwing the eggs . . .

Story #36: Model Rocketry

The stupidest thing that we ever did involved model rocketry. This was not just some run-of-the-mill retardedness, but real serious "Thank God it didn't work" stupidity. Here's how it went down.

Around Grade 10, one of the shop teachers in our school started a model rocketry club, which Sandy and I immediately signed up for. Now this sounded awesome, as what could be better than building rockets and firing them off? Well it turned out that building a rocket was actually much harder than it looked. Over in our local mall was a store called "The Hobby Shop" that sold miscellaneous, over-priced crap to teenagers and old nerds. One of the items they stocked were model rocket kits. Now the difference between the cover picture of the intricately

detailed rocket zooming across the cosmos, and the junk that you actually got inside the box was stark. All they gave you were a couple of waxed-up toilet paper tubes, a bit of balsa wood, and a one-page poorly mimeographed instruction sheet. One mis-step and your rocket was aerodynamically unstable. Glue the balsa fins on slightly crooked, and the thing would spin out of control. Sand the nose cone too little, and the parachute wouldn't come out, causing your $25 rocket to head into the ground at high-speed. Anyway - you get the picture.

Now the way model rocketry worked, was that you set a launch day a couple of months into the future, and then all the junior nerds set about constructing their rockets, and painting them with whatever they could get their hands on. A couple of mine were finished off with Sears WeatherBeater exterior paint, as the cost of a little can of model paint was far too exorbitant. When they were done, you essentially had this painted toilet paper tube stuffed with a parachute made from a plastic garbage bag, a balsa nose-cone that attached to the toilet paper tube with an elastic, and a hole in the bottom in which you placed the rocket engine. To launch this beast, there was a piece of plastic straw glued to the outside of the rocket, that you placed over a length of straightened coat-hanger. Igniting the rocket involved connecting a car battery to a piece of nichrome wire[†] coated with some chemical that burned when the wire got hot.

Once the appointed day arrived, we all collected our rockets and headed out to the range to blast off. Surprisingly, Dad came along to a couple of these events as well - primarily because I suspect he just enjoyed

---

[†] The stuff electric stove elements are made of.

watching some kid's rocket nose-dive into the dirt at high-speed.

Now there were two kinds of rocket engines - ones that were for single-stage rockets, and another for multi-stage rockets. The first kind burned for a bit and then blew some gas out the top to kick off the nose-cone and parachute. The second kind shot fire upwards to ignite the second stage.

After watching some kid's two stage rocket go crazy and explode - it hit us like a thunderbolt - why bother with any parachute? Just fill a rocket up with gun-powder, glue the nose-cone on, and then glue a first stage engine in.[†]

Later that summer, we were finally ready for a trial of the concept at our proving grounds behind the nearby Sears warehouse. We piled onto our bicycles, bringing a rocket, a coat-hanger, and a car-battery. On a warm August evening, the rocket ascended rapidly into the sky, where it proceeded to turn into a fire-ball. Wow! OK - so it wasn't the hoped-for explosion, but it was still pretty cool: until the fireball descended into the tall grass about a 1/4 mile away and started a brush-fire! Aaah! If we burned down the Sears warehouse, we'd catch some serious trouble when we got home. We got onto our bikes, pedalling furiously to get to the fire before it got out of control. Fortunately, after about 10 minutes of stamping and totally melting our running shoes, we were able to put it out.

OK - back to the drawing board on the gun-powder mixture, but the basic idea was proven.

[†] We used Estes C-60 engines as they were the biggest you could get in Ottawa.

Next spring at the next launch we were ready with three "warheads." The plan was to try and nail a truck on the highway with one. Thank God that they came up short. We tilted the launch rod down low to "compensate" for the wind, and off they went, where they all exploded with little puffs of white smoke out towards the highway. We were able to cover up the explosions, as some other kids had started dumping baby-powder into their parachute area which produced a similar effect.

Again - stupid as hell, and thank God we hit nothing. Even we, on the way home realized we were complete morons . . .

Story #37: Corn Syrup

One day in grade 11, while experimenting with the physical properties of clear corn syrup, it occurred to me that this stuff would be perfect on a stair railing at school. Packing up a little container of the syrup, I confided my plan to Sandy who immediately saw its genius. At lunch we headed to one of the main stairwells and waited until it was empty. While Sandy kept watch, I opened the container and drizzled a nice bead of corn syrup down the railing. Then we headed back up the stairs and loitered around waiting to see the effect of my scheme. We were expecting disgust from unsuspecting fools as they slid their hands down the railing and felt the sticky syrup, but instead we were surprised when some cool grade 10 kid decided to slide down the doctored railing on his butt. Instead of encountering the normal sliding friction which would allow him to gracefully descend and jump off at the bottom, he instead encountered significantly reduced sliding friction, and proceeded down the railing at warp speed, shooting off the end of the railing into the wall, with his ass covered in corn syrup. He didn't suffer any serious injuries, so it was a successful prank. Plus we learned that despite its

viscosity, corn syrup can function quite well as a lubricant for pants.

4.7 More High-School Stories

Dear Reader, Just to demonstrate my good faith to you, and to perhaps dispel any misgivings you may have about wasting money on this fine tome, I will leave you with two other stories involving my high-school years that I hope you find interesting.

Story #38: Reader's Digest

Throughout my high-school years I was an avid reader, typically going through two paper-backs per day, illicitly reading through every class, with the book hidden below the surface of my desk (similar to how kids today use their cell phones). Unfortunately, my tastes were confined to adventure, Sci-Fi, and fantasy, which made using my voracious book throughput of rather limited use when it came to English class. To my unceasing annoyance, our English department seemed to be very prejudiced against these genres, and instead forced me to read works with no real literary value such as Romeo and Juliet, 1984, Moby Dick, Heart of Darkness, etc. . . Consequently, instead of getting credit for all of my reading, I was instead being forced to read books I hated. To make matters worse, I was also being forced to read another 12 books per semester, of which only two could be in the "Other" category.

At this point, you the Reader may ask "So what's the big deal? Just suck it up and read some different books!" Wrong! Like Solzhenitsyn, I would never willingly accept the yoke of literary oppression, and would fight until my dying breath for freedom. With this iron conviction in my heart, I turned to my secret weapon - the Reader's Digest.

Now this magazine today would typically be found in your Grandmother's bathroom, or on the table in an oncologist's office, but back in pre-Internet days it had a much broader circulation, and my Mom was naturally a subscriber. This saccharine melange of uplifting stories and corny jokes would head straight into our bathroom every month, where it would proudly take its place on the counter next to the toilet, relegating the old, beat up issue to the top of the toilet tank. In addition to providing old people around North America with a valuable source of back-up toilet paper, the Reader's Digest also afforded the subscriber the ability to receive on a quarterly basis, a hard-bound issue of "Reader's Digest Condensed Books".

Now to my understanding, back in the day there was a lot of pressure to seem educated and "with the times" by reading hot, new books, and with humans being human, a market existed for short versions of "worthwhile" books, in which enough meat was left to make it seem like you read the whole book, without actually having to put in the effort. This, dear Reader, was my secret weapon!

Unfortunately, there was one little hitch: the bibliography. In order to be able to leverage the work the Reader's Digest's team of "abridgers" had done, I needed to get an actual copy of the real book to get the details for the bibliography- something that unfortunately proved to be a lot harder than I initially thought. You see, my Mom's collection of "Reader's Digest Condensed Books", consisted of about 75% really new books that my school library didn't have a copy of, or old books. The end result was that I probably spent more time trying to find 10 old books in our library that were "condensed", than if I just read books myself.

Story #39: The Swords

The high-school I went to in Ottawa had some trade-school courses - one of which was machine-shop. I liked building things, and also found I was pretty good at it, so over the next 4 years I earned a fair degree of respect from my machine-shop teacher. Consequently, in my final year of high-school (yes Grade 13[†]), I decided it was time to make a serious weapon.

Plan "A" was a steel cross-bow. I had seen a few movies featuring these, and it struck me as the perfect high-school project[‡]. Unfortunately, my machine-shop teacher did not see things the same way, and promptly vetoed it. Damn!

"So what would be OK?" I asked. After fishing through the usual items, such as sniper rifles, grenades, etc. I got the OK on a sword.

"Not too bad, I can work with that" I thought.

Over the next few days, I spent all of my free library time studying swords, sword construction, sword types, optimal blade angles, etc. and at the end came up with two swords: a two-handed crusader's sword, and it's arch-foe - the scimitar[*].

The next step was to procure some steel that could be hardened, and since my options were effectively limited by what the only steel-supply place in Ottawa had to offer[††], I

[†] Yeah - laugh it up Douchebags! Ontario up until 1988 still had Grade 13!!

[‡] As I'm sure you, the Reader, will agree.

[*] I was also into Dungeons and Dragons at the time, so the swords fit nicely into my warped milieu.

[††]The magic of an "Internet-free" existence.

settled on something called 8650 steel. This could be hardened, didn't break my budget (which was pretty thin), and was apparently used to make snow-plow blades.

Over the next year, I proceeded to burn-up milling machine cutters (much to my machine-shop teacher's chagrin, as the steel was tough to work), and through a seemingly endless amount of grinding and filing (and a serious hydraulic press to bend the scimitar) I managed to create the two swords.

The next steps were to harden them, and create hilts. OK - so hardening a sword is not exactly easy. I know you are supposed to heat it white-hot and then quench it in the heart of a red-headed boy, but not having access to red-heads of any sort, I hadn't a clue how this was going to be achieved. However! I did have a plan formulated with regards to the hilt.

Over my years of science class, I had noticed that the chrome retort-stand rods[†] (which were frequently broken off at the base by negligent fools such as myself) were made of brass. And I also observed that down the hall in the ceramics studio there was a kiln that supposedly went up to 2000°F - more than enough to melt brass. Furthermore, for some God-unbeknownest reason, the science teacher kept the broken brass rods. Bingo! I would melt the brass in the kiln and then pour it into plaster moulds to make the hilts.

After getting approval from the science teacher to re-appropriate the broken retort-stand rods, I proceeded to strip the chrome plating off them in our machine-shop with

---

[†] The chrome rod things that you screwed into the lab counter so you could attach beakers to them to do things like heating their contents with a bunsen burner.

a lathe and a bastard file. Next I made the wooden blanks of the hilts I wanted, and from there made the moulds in which to cast the brass castings using drywall plaster[†], which essentially doomed the casting exercise from the start.

Anyway, as they say "Long story, short" - the casting process was a train-wreck: the art-kiln was not really up to 2000°F, despite its thermometer claiming to the contrary. Consequently, the first melt of the brass rods worked, but in the process the heating elements in the kiln burned up. Then when I poured the molten brass into the moulds, they proceeded to boil, resulting in a Swiss-cheese-like casting that was total garbage[‡].

OK - well, whatever, I'd figure the casting thing out later. In the meantime, I found out that the father of a girl who sat behind me in one of my math classes worked at Canada's National Research Council (NRC) machine shop, and volunteered to harden my swords for me. YAY!!

[†] WHAT! You the informed reader may be thinking, and you are correct! Disaster loometh. Sadly the 1958 version of the Encylopedia Americana that we owned and the more extensive Encyclopedia Britannica in my school did not adequately cover the perils that would result from trying to use drywall plaster as a mould compound for casting brass, and yeah, I get it. Even a simple fool would have selected Plaster-of-Paris. Drywall plaster is hygroscopic meaning that you can never really dry it out. Plus it dramatically shrinks when it dries resulting in cracking, etc.

[‡] When testing my Crusader's sword blank for drawing over the shoulder, from a back-mounted scabbard, I had found it was too long. Consequently, I cut the end off to make it drawable, and turned the remaining piece into an SAS-style boot knife. These were the only usable pieces from my entire effort - solely because they were small enough and didn't suffer the Swiss cheesing the other pieces did.

I turned over my swords to her, and a week later they came back hardened, with a blackened finish. Unfortunately, my Crusader's sword also had a 10° bend in it, and it was like an unstraightenable spring. I bent the thing 90° and "Choing!" - it went back to exactly how it was. And then depression set in.

Several years later in university, I watched the movie Excalibur, and when the Lady of The Lake caught the sword, the music swelled, and the sun set, I was on fire. I HAD TO FINISH THE SWORDS!!!!!

I was now in 3rd year university, and presumably a little bit smarter. I phoned up the NRC machine-shop and explained my plight. Fortunately, the guys there remembered my swords from 3 years ago, and even though my friend's Dad had retired, one of his co-workers agreed to try and fix the sword. With some great skill, and an oxy-acetylene torch, he straightened the blade, requenched it, Gabriel's trumpet sounded from heaven: the blade was straight, and Saladin was to be vanquished!

The next step was to deal with the hilts. Digging through the Yellow Pages, I found a business named Carleton Brass that claimed to do brass castings. Throwing my close-to-penniless ass on their mercy, they agreed to do a casting of my dusty wooden hilt blanks for about $80. It was total charity, but it worked.

Over the next month, I polished, and filed the hilts into their final shape, and then with a propane torch[†], soldered them into place.

[†] It was my Dad's house - no such thing as an oxy-acetylene torch there

I then finished the swords with some oak grips, wrapped them with criss-cross kid-leather[†], and at 1:00am on a hot summer night, headed outside with my Crusader's sword and proceeded to attack our crab-apple tree on the front lawn.

Each slash of the sharpened sword resulted in a satisfying "Ching!" as a Mohammedan branch fell to the ground[‡]. Like a whirling Dervish, I brought the tree to its knees. Then - Saints be Praised! - I heard the sound of a Satanic motorcycle coming down the street. "Justice will be served!" I thought, as I jumped into the path of the oncoming motorcycle, sword held high.

The poor bastard swerved around me, gunned the motorcycle, and vanished into the night.

Smiling, I went to bed, feeling the power of my sword[*].

[†] I found some leather supply place in downtown Ottawa that basically gave me some scraps that I used.

[‡] OK, a lot of my good friends are Muslim, but at the time, holding a Crusader's sword, made by my own hand - you have to cut me some slack for synthetic religious fanaticism.

[*] Saladin's I finished next, to the chagrin of the crab-apple tree.

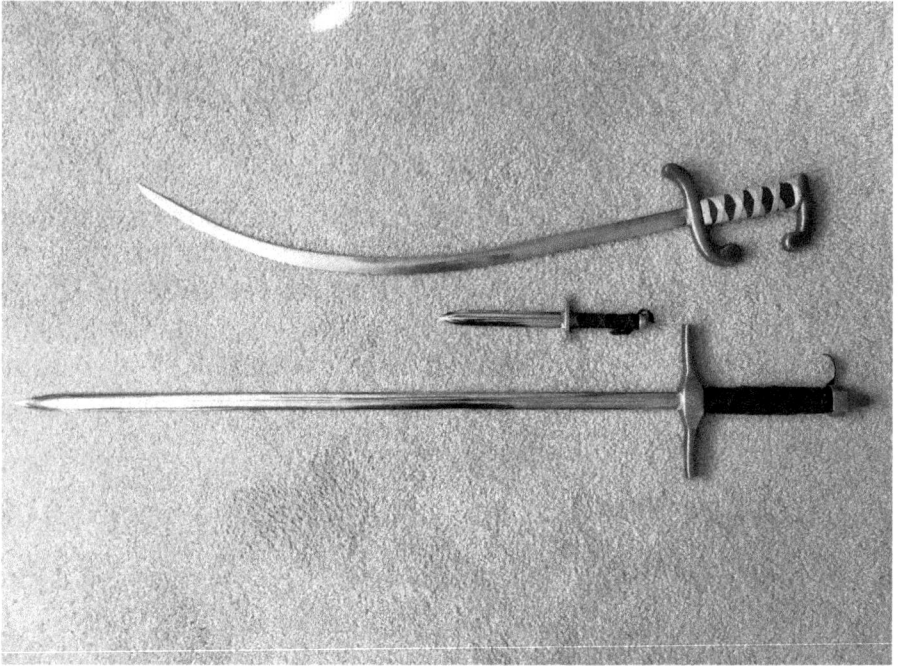

Figure 4.2 **The swords**

After I moved out of the house, I was somewhat free of the day-to-day shenanigans that used to fill our daily lives. My brother and Dad continued to ruin each other's showers for years after, but I was no longer directly involved. Instead what happened were long periods of quiet, interspersed by some very amusing and elaborate stunts - most of which involved the written word. Before I head there, I want to regale you with one quick but humorous food incident.

Story #40: The Grey Hotdogs

My brother couldn't cook anything to save his life. To this very day, most of what he eats comes out of a can or a box.[†] One Sunday afternoon, I popped by my parents house to visit, and grab a snack. My brother was in the basement watching TV, and my parents were gone. Rooting through the freezer, I found the traditional staple of my family growing up: hotdogs. I checked that there was bread, and then proceeded to pry off a couple of frozen hot-dogs to boil them in water. While in the process of this culinary magic, my brother comes running upstairs in a panic.

"Stop - that's my lunch!" he yelled, eyes blazing.

"What's the problem? Make something else - there's eggs, salame, cheese - all sorts of stuff," I replied.

[†] When he got married, I bought him a Ronco® "Hot Diggity Dogger" which was essentially a toaster for two hot-dogs and two buns. (It seems that they still sell them to this day).

The "Letter Guy" and Other Stories

"I don't know how to cook anything else," Dave admitted sheepishly, as he went back downstairs, reassured that his hotdogs were safe from my depredations.

"Don't know how to cook anything else . . ." Immediately a plan formed in my brain. Downstairs in the remnants of my chemistry lab, I recalled that I had a block of grey modelling clay. Springing into action, I ran downstairs, grabbed the clay and proceeded to fashion three grey hotdogs. Replacing Dave's treasured hotdogs in the wrapper with these colorless grey babies, I stashed the real hotdogs downstairs in the freezer chest. I then set about to make scrambled eggs and left.

That evening, I heard how a hungry Dave came upstairs later that afternoon to make himself "lunch," and instead of finding the expected hotdogs, he found frosty, grey hotdogs. He tells me he almost puked with revulsion, thinking they had somehow gone bad.

5.1 Edwin

This next section is dedicated to my father, Edwin. Edwin is a unique tortured individual who has the guilty conscience of a Lutheran sinner, but the soul of a clown. His worst nightmare was to do something that would make him stand out, or even worse be judged to be a bad neighbor. Our lawn was always perfectly cut, and our house perfectly painted in tasteful black and white, and everything was "perfect" - all the time. Anything out of place was immediately put right. Despite this striving for respectability, attention and embarrassment stalked him relentlessly.

When I was 17, I bought a 1974 2.8L Ford Capri and proceeded to tear it apart and rebuild it in my Dad's driveway. What started out as a "couple of weeks of quick

Figure 5.1 **The gutted 1974 Ford Capri**

repair" turned into a year-long journey through purgatory for my Dad. Every morning he'd look out the front window and see this primer and Bondo covered shell on axle jacks - no doors, engine, nothing. His lifetime of striving for middle-class anonymity with a lawn that would be admired

for its quiet perfection was in vain with this eyesore of a vehicle that he despaired would never move again. He offered several times to buy it out just so he could have it towed off. No such luck - this was my dream vehicle and there was no way I was letting it go. Plus it had no wheels, so he wasn't even sure how to remove it.

He also fared poorly under pressure. For instance, if he was in a restaurant when a waiter would try and take his order and he wasn't ready, he would panic and order random things (usually items he hated), and then would be too embarassed to recant his order, even if there was time.

Story #43: The Car Dealership

One day, my Mom and Dad decided to start looking for a new car. A salesman began showing them vehicles on the showroom floor. On one that looked promising, the salesman opened the hood to show my father the engine and left them to look at the vehicle. After a few minutes of looking, they were done, and my father decided to close the hood. Expecting the hood to be on a spring, like standard 1960's and 1970's American cars, he pushed it down to close it. Unfortunately it was a foreign vehicle with a rod that you lifted up to prop the hood open, and instead of closing, the hood promptly folded in half. Mom instantly beetled off to the other side of the showroom to put as much distance between herself and my erstwhile father who at this point she had never met before in her life, while he, beet-red, started searching for the salesman - or any salesman for that matter. It turned out that the car dealership had insurance for this sort of thing, and it was not that much of a disaster, but it sure embarrassed my Dad.

Story #44: The Desk

Another time, my Dad was looking at kitchen accessories, and he found one that had a retractable surface on a spring. My father squatted down to see how it worked and whilst mucking with it, it sprang out. He fell over backwards with the desk on top of him. On returning home, my father felt the need to unburden his soul and promptly confessed to rolling around in the aisle of the store under the desk, whilst shocked customers watched.

Story #45: Cunning Stunts

If you put a few drinks into my Dad, the clown inside him would start to emerge, and he would start to tell jokes. One particular favorite of his was "What's the difference between a beauty pageant and a circus routine?" The answer is supposed to be "One features an array of cunning stunts," but inevitably he would say "One features an array of stunning c*nts." Twice I heard him tell this at formal events and it would immediately stop all conversation in the room, with everyone staring in shocked horror at my beet-red father. He would then start trying to explain how the joke was supposed to go, which just made those in the immediate vicinity wish they were somewhere else.

Story #46: Herman and Horst

My Dad's oldest sister lived in Saskatchewan, and had previously been married to a German man named Herman and was now married to a Prussian named Horst. Inevitably, my Dad would mix up the names and call Horst Herman - which pissed Horst off and embarrassed my father. To help matters along whenever we visited his sister, Dave and I would start in on the approach to the house with the following dialogue:

Paul: "OK Dad - remember it's Horst, and NOT Hermann. What ever you do, do not think about Herman!"

Dave: "Yeah Dad. No Herman, don't say Herman, don't think about Herman."

Mom: "You mutts! Stop it!"

Paul: "OK - just don't say Herman. You remember how mad Horst was last time you said it."

(at this point Dad is starting to panic as we are a couple of blocks away and he feels the noose tightening)

When we finally get to the door, the first thing out of my Dad's mouth is "Hi Herman!"

Story #47: Potatoes and Tomatoes

Back in the day, we had a garden full of tomatoes on one end, and potatoes on the other. My Mom sent my Dad out to get some potatoes, and as you the reader will probably surmise, Edwin returned about 5 minutes later with both hands full of tomato plants, wondering why they had produced no potatoes. This resulted in him being berated for being a fool by my Mom.

Story #48: The Round-Robin

Back in the days before e-mail, the internet, and cheap long-distance, people had to write letters. Furthermore, if you came from a large family, instead of writing the same thing to all of your brothers and sisters, what you did was something called a round-robin letter. Everybody wrote about what was happening in their life, and sent it on to the next sibling, so that it went in a circle. Well that's all fine and dandy as long as you don't mix up your round-robin

letter with a personal letter complaining to your brother about your oldest sister - which is exactly what happened to my Dad one day. The chill from that took years to dissipate.

As a humourous follow-up, during the chill years, Dave and I created another round-robin letter that was far worse, and had subliminal messages about her oldest son being a failure written very lightly in pencil behind the otherwise boring ink. Fortunately, this letter was discovered by my Dad prior to the sealing of the envelope. I guess after this he started double-checking the contents.

Story #49: The Door Lock

After I left home, my room was essentially used as a storage area, with nothing much happening in there. From this, the germ of an idea to torture my Dad sprang, as the idea of anything in his house being out of his control drove him mental. The plan involved an old keyed door-knob from our front-door which he had replaced, and was now sitting in a drawer in his workshop in the basement along with the only keys to it.

One weekend when I was going out of town on a Friday, and my parents and brother were returning a day later from vacation, I went over to their house and switched the door-knob on my old bedroom door with the old keyed front-door-knob. I then locked the lock, took the keys, left a note on the door saying "Gone away for the weekend, will be back on Sunday with the keys," and left.

According to my brother and Mom, after they returned home, my Dad lasted about 20 minutes before he got a pry-bar out and broke down the door. Even though there was nothing of any value, nor any other reason to go into

the room, he couldn't survive knowing it was locked and him unable to enter for 24 hours.

Story #50: The Outaouais

The region of greater Ottawa consists of several cities and is split across the Ottawa river, with one side in Ontario, and the other side (primarily being Hull) in Quebec. The entire region on the Quebec side is also known as the Outaouais (pronounced "Ooo-ta-way" - it's a French name, so to an English speaker I expect the reaction to be "Seriously??"). Anyway, on almost every news broadcast you hear this name mentioned, and everyone knows what it is, and most know roughly how to spell it. Apparently though, my Dad was not one of them, as one day I was over at my parent's house and my Dad was reading the paper and asked "Where is this Ooo-ya-too-sis place?". This resulted in him being berated for being a fool by my Mom.

Story #51: The Lawn

My Dad and I are continuously at each other when it pertains to our houses and especially our lawns. A typical exchange goes like this:

Edwin sends me a picture of something outside - like how beautiful the flowers on their front yard are, or some such thing.

PAUL: "Wow - that really looks beautiful. Ottawa really is lovely in the summer time. By the way though, what's up with the lawn by the hedges?"

EDWIN: (concerned) "What do you mean?"

PAUL: "You know, that spot by the hedges. It looks slightly brown. Have you been watering it enough?"

EDWIN: "Get out of here! There's nothing wrong with the lawn. You're just making this up!"

PAUL: "No seriously - look. It's like it isn't as healthy. Maybe there are cinch bugs living there?"

EDWIN: (squints at the photograph, clutching onto the belief that I am just teasing him, but as always, a niggling concern that maybe I'm not) "I don't see anything! You're seeing things."

PAUL: (acquiescing) "Yeah - you're right. It's probably nothing. Sorry - I just thought I saw something".

This is precisely the worst thing I could say to Edwin, as it now left him with doubts as to the health of his lawn. This would then result in him heading outside to contrast the color in the spot I was talking about with the rest of the lawn, and if you stared at something long enough like this, you could convince yourself that it really was a slightly different color. This would then lead to pulling up chunks of grass to try and catch the dreaded cinch bug - which would typically not be there.

However, every once in a while, I would luck into being right, setting things up for next time.

Story #52: Groundhogs

When I would show up at my parents house, I would often tease my Dad that I thought I saw a groundhog in his backyard. Now these furry devils are pretty much the king of lawn pests[†]. They love to chew on anything green, and

---

[†] After deer, which are the ultimate lawn and garden nightmare, to which all of your landscape (including rose bushes) looks like the salad bar at an all-you-can-eat buffet.

will happily tunnel into your lawn, leaving unsightly piles of dirt, with a devastated lawn and garden soon to follow.

The first time I teased him about this, he panicked and went tearing off out of the house, hoping to scare the phantom groundhog away. Of course nothing would be there, and upon returning to the house, he would immediately suspect that I had either been mistaken or made the whole thing up. I never cracked and told him that I was just jacking with him, and only admitted that maybe I was mistaken. Eventually he started to ignore my periodic provocations and I started to "see" less and less "groundhogs". Then one day, a real groundhog showed up, with no help whatsoever from me!

Unfortunately I was no longer living in Ottawa, so I couldn't come to watch the festivities, but I heard about them in detail from both my Dad and his brother Garry who happened to be visiting at the time. Apparently a groundhog decided to stake a homestead claim on my Dad's sidelawn, and after digging out his burrow, settled in for a long stay. Imagine my Dad's horror when he came out to the driveway and sees a furry butt scampering into a hole beside a mound of fresh earth on his sidelawn. A hole visible to the whole street. A hole clearly indicative of major lawn issues. A hole which devalued real-estate in the whole neighborhood, and which was clearly his responsibility!

The first (and usually futile) plan of attack when dealing with groundhogs, is to attempt to encourage the furry devil to relocate by filling his hole in with rock. With my Dad the result was as expected: next morning the rock was dug out, and a new back-door to the hole installed.

The usual second plan of attack is to flood the hole, making it unpleasant and muddy. Again with my Dad, no luck, and next morning a side door to the hole was installed.

The final plan of attack (my father didn't have the heart to kill the groundhog) was to get a cage and some carrot bait. This actually worked, and soon the groundhog accepted a corporate relocation package to a field 10 miles away.

Story #53: Glucifer

My Dad was always a bit of a hypochondriac. He assiduously exercised, had a cholesterol level close to zero, and any time some sort of health finding would show up about something being potentially bad for you, he'd immediately eliminate it from his diet. At one point in the 1980's, aluminum was suspected of contributing to Alzheimer's, so out went deodorant and aluminum cookware (apparently the threat of divorce outweighed the dangers of aluminum sulphate, so the ban on deodorant was only temporary). Same with caffeine, resulting in morning coffee being replaced with hot water - something I routinely teased him about, until I found myself actually enjoying it throughout the day years later.

Well one year, my Dad (probably courtesy of the Reader's Digest Book of Disease) starts thinking that he has celiac disease, and can no longer tolerate gluten which is found in wheat. We are skeptical, but to our surprise he actually tests positive for celiac[†]. This immediately results in a purge of my parent's house, with any substance that could possibly contain wheat being expunged[‡].

[†] I am frankly still skeptical about the diagnosis, but it makes him happy, so whatever . . .

[‡] My Dad loved cleaning, and "If in doubt - throw it out" was his motto.

From my perspective, the deletion of flour from my parent's house really didn't change things that much, as on a scale of 1 to 10, where 1 is "awful", and 10 is "terrible", Mom's cooking continued to clock in at around a 5 (OK - I'm being a dick, as her cooking at this point was not that bad). Consequently, all that really happened is that my brother and I just added teasing Dad about gluten into our repertoire. An example of this is as follows:

PAUL: (looking at the ingredients label on some salami while my Dad eats lunch) "Hey Dad! Does wheat flour contain gluten?"

EDWIN: (immediately concerned) "What - where are you reading that??"

PAUL: "It's towards the end of the ingredients list on this salami. You're not eating this are you?"

EDWIN: (grabs the salami from me and carefully scans the ingredients, and with relief finds no "Wheat Flour") "You jerk!"

Years later, while living in California, my parents came to visit, and during a trip to the grocery store to buy some gluten-free flour for cooking during their visit, I was surprised to see that they actually sold bags of gluten. Being the dick that I am, I promptly bought a bag of each, and the awesome part was that the only apparent difference between them was the title on the bag. Otherwise, they were indistinguishable!

After my parents arrived, I start teasing my Dad.

PAUL: "Dad - check this out. We even bought this gluten-free flour for you"

EDWIN: (looks at the bags, and his face goes white) "This is a bag of gluten!!"

PAUL: "No way! They're both gluten-free flour . . . Oh my God - you're right! I must have grabbed a bag of gluten by accident! Wow - I'll have to make sure that we don't mix them up"

EDWIN: (stunned and confused): "Why would they sell such a thing?

PAUL: "Why not? Lots of people enjoy gluten. I know I do."

The effect was hilarious, much like Superman finding a breakfast cereal made out of kryptonite. Over the next couple of days, the bag of gluten followed me around, and kept inadvertently "turning up". At night I would tape it to the guest bedroom door, much like sealing a vampire in his tomb with garlic and a cross. Finally I drew a face on it, and started calling it Glucifer.

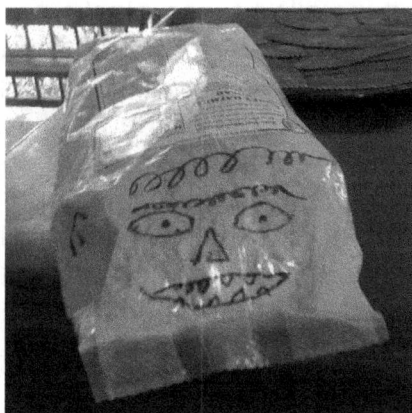

Figure 5.2 **Glucifer**

To this day, we still greet my Dad with "Gluten Tag Edwin!".

5.2 More Dave Stories

These next few stories are in the transition period when I was in university or just after I left home, and Dave was still living at home.

Story #54: The Curtains

I included this next story at my brother's request, as I had forgotten about it. In my fourth year of university, my brother was finishing Grade 13, and he had a hell of a time with calculus, which I happened to be good at. Consequently, in order to do his homework, he was forced to sit in the living room and ask me questions while I did my homework on the other couch, sitting near the lovely gold drapes which adorned our front windows. Underneath every window in a 1960's house in Canada was a register (aka heating vent on the floor) which was supposed to keep the ice off the crappy old sliding panes of glass these houses were originally build with[†]. Since all of these windows had long been replaced with proper windows, there was no reason to keep them warm, and as a result, my Mom had installed these plastic register deflectors to keep the air from going up behind the curtains. Now the drapes were long, and if you didn't close them properly, they'd sit crooked on top of the plastic deflectors, versus hanging in stately elegance behind them. One day, whilst helping my mathematically challenged sibling, I noticed him get up from across the room and flip the drapery off the plastic deflector, about 5' from where I was sitting. As soon as he sat down, I got up and put the drape back on top of the deflector. Muttering "You dick!", he again got up and

---

[†] Pearson "sliders" which consisted of two panes of glass in a wooden slot, that slid back and forth. You locked them closed with a latching knob that shoved one pane against the other. When it hit -30°F outside you'd get a 1/4" of ice on the bottom of these, which would then melt and start to rot the wooden frame.

"fixed" the drape. I couldn't believe that he was stupid enough to expose this phobia to me, his caring brother. I immediately went down the hall, and got the floor attachment from the vacuum cleaner so that I could flip the drape back on top of the air deflector without having to get up. Soon Dave was rolling around on the couch in agony, knowing that the drapes were not properly situated, and that any attempt to fix them would result in my immediately un-doing it. Plus he couldn't really do anything to me, or I wouldn't help him with his homework.

Finally Dave could take it no more. He yelled downstairs "Mom - Dad, Paul is bothering me and I can't do my homework!". My Dad came trudging upstairs, and when he heard Dave's complaint just laughed and called him a loser. Totally unexpected, and very gratifying.

Story #55: The Short Sheet

This is a classic prank that seems to have fallen into disfavor. I became aware of it through watching old reruns like "Sergeant Bilko" and "F-Troop" and always wondered what it was. Finally I asked an uncle who explained it to me: basically you take the top bed sheet and fold it in half horizontally so that the fold is half-way down the bed. Then you tuck the lower part of the sheet under the mattress, and wait for Morpheus to call your unsuspecting victim to bed. The result is an apparently normal bed that prevents your victim from extending his legs more than half-way down the bed. If your victim is especially tired, this prank is extra fun, as you basically have to remake the entire bed to get the top sheet into place properly.

With Dave things went extra well, as I sabotaged his bed when I knew he would be at his weakest. He had joined the Canadian Military Reserves and had been on exercise for the weekend at Petawawa (a mosquito-infested swamp /

military base in northern Ontario where Ottawa reserve regiments often went on maneuvers) and I knew would be dead-tired after basically 48 hours of no sleep. Sure enough, he was dead-tired, and after staggering around eating some leftovers, ditching his uniform in the laundry, etc. he headed to bed. Since my bedroom was across the hall from his, I made sure I was there to enjoy the spectacle. After about 1 minute, the show started. It began with some struggling noises, followed by a "What the hell?" and then some more struggling. Finally a light turned on in his room, and after some archaeology on the bed, Dave began to suspect that what had happened to the sheets was not just bad luck, but active sabotage by his arch-nemesis: Paul. I feigned sleep, but he was immediately in my room and turned on the light.

"You douche! What did you do to my bed?" yelled my tired and confused brother. Apparently he still didn't really figure out what had happened, so I explained the genius of it, and gave him a tour. Once he understood, it became a whole lot funnier. Next night we short-sheeted our parent's bed.

Story #56: The Old Canadian $2 Bill

My brother was an avid Canadian currency collector and had a large collection of old coins and bank-notes. He was paranoid about the collection, and would have stupid dreams like going to the coin shop to buy an old $5 bill from the 1950's and upon returning home found it had turned into a toothbrush. One of the worst experiences of his life was when one of my Dad's uncles, who was also a coin collector died, and left Dad a bunch of his collection. My Dad viewed the whole thing as a cash windfall, and didn't give a rat's-ass about any collectible value. He promptly took his inheritance to the Sears Coin Shop and unloaded it for whatever the guy gave him. Over the next decade, my brother wound up buying most of it back, at vastly inflated

prices. He is still pissed to this very day about this! Anyway - I have provided you, the reader, with the appropriate backdrop, and you are now in the right frame of mind for this next story.

One day, I happened upon an old Canadian $2 bill from the 1950's. It wasn't in mint condition, but it wasn't bad, so I offered to sell it to my brother for some outrageous mark-up. Since he already had a good one, he declined, whereupon I promptly ripped it in half. It was like a punch in the gut for him!

"You dick!! Why did you do that??" he demanded.

"You didn't want it, and I'm just going to spend it, so who cares if it has some tape on it?" I replied with a smirk. In his mind I was now a sociopath.

Story #57: Altered Coins

In a job at a startup, we had to implement some plating processes to coat copper printed circuit board traces with a tin surface finish for soldering, and also had to implement a gold plating process[†]. Once we got this up and running, I immediately tried to see what a new penny would look like coated with tin. It was awesome, and it looked like aluminum. Ha! Dave wandered into my sights, as I cranked out a few more aluminum pennies.

That weekend, I stopped by my parents, and showed Dave the "new" aluminum pennies. He was stunned! Somehow he had missed this breaking numismatic story about Canada switching the new production of pennies over to half aluminum on the way to a permanent transition next

---

[†] I suspect it is not so cool to do this anymore as the chemical disposal was less than controlled.

year, to save money. It was total crap that I had made up, but without Internet, there wasn't an easy way of verifying this without phoning the government, or going to a coin-shop. A few days later, and a lot of phoning, Dave was convinced that I had doctored the coins. He was still impressed.

As a follow-up to this story, a few months later, I gold-plated a few new quarters (which were gold, but looked like new bronze) and slipped them into my Dad's change, knowing he'd spot them and show Dave. It again worked perfectly, and with no obvious "Paul involvement" Dave again went on a wild goose chase.

Story #58: Testicle Cancer

As I mentioned in an earlier story, my mother subscribed to the Reader's Digest magazine, and also received on a quarterly basis a "Reader's Digest Condensed Book". What I didn't mention, was that at one point in the 1970's she also received a Reader's Digest bonus book that my brother and I referred to as "The Reader's Digest Book of Disease"[†]. Of course my brother and I immediately became fascinated with this book, avidly reading about nasty tropical parasites, legendary diseases like "Cat Scratch Fever", and generally trying to find the most horrible disease listed. While this provided lots of fodder for attacks of hypochondria[‡], I eventually grew tired of it, and moved on to other things. Not so my brother Dave.

One day at work, I get this anguished call from my brother:

[†] Digging around on Google, it appears that this was probably the 1976 Reader's Digest book "Family Health Guide and Medical Encyclopedia", but I'm not 100% sure, as may parent's copy has long vanished.

[‡] Maybe that wasn't just a mosquito bite, but was actually the onset of elephantiasis!

DAVE: "Paul - I think I have testicle cancer!"

PAUL: "What??? Have you seen a doctor??"

DAVE: "No"

PAUL: "Well how do you know you have it?"

DAVE: "Because one of my balls is swollen on the end"

PAUL: "So how come you think that means you have testicle cancer?"

DAVE: "Because that's the symptom in the Reader's Digest Book of Disease"

PAUL: "IDIOT! Stop looking at that thing, and go see a doctor!"

Next week, Dave goes to the doctor and reports back to me that, Saints be Praised, he in fact does not have testicle cancer, and all is fine.

PAUL: ""So what was it?"

DAVE: (sheepishly answering) "My testicle was swollen was because of too many self-examinations, and I'm supposed to stop it."

5.3 The Written Word

It turns out that the ultimate prank involves a letter. I know it's old-school, and the idea that something can turn up in your mailbox and torture you seems ridiculous, but it's true. Think about it: if it has an official air to it, there is almost no way to immediately rebut or debunk it unless you pick up the phone, and if it is designed properly, a phone call will yield no immediate satisfaction. It's perfect. So without further ado, here are three humourous stories.

Story #59: My Heartbroken Godmother

I don't know what I did to my brother to deserve this little gem, but it was an arrow that pierced my cynical armor and struck its mark with uncanny accuracy[†]. For some reason (and I'm not actually sure why), I decided to start corresponding with my godmother, a woman named Dorothy R. She was an old friend of my mother's and I remember her telling me that she was all alone, and often asked how her godson was doing. Perhaps feeling human emotions, I decided to reach out and write her a letter to try and connect with her. I was in my early twenties and doing reasonably well, so I thought it would make her happy to hear I was doing OK.

I wrote the first letter introducing myself to her, and telling her about my life. She immediately happily responded, telling me about her life, and then "Tag - you're it" it was back to me. OK - I was now out of things to say after the first letter, and the fact her reply came back to me after 2 weeks terrified me. "What the hell more can I say to her?" Well she did ask a bunch of questions, so I figured, I can

---

[†] Yeah, yeah . . . you the vicarious reader in your comfortable bed or armchair, with your glass of brandy, or whatever, have already decided that I am an unredeemable douche-bag and deserve anything that is coming to me. Maybe you're right . . .

at least answer them. Getting my writing pad out, with the lines visible through the paper, I started off "Dear godmother Dorothy . . ." and dutifully answered her questions. To try and slow her down, I tried to limit my questions - I mean what was I supposed to say? "How is your life in northern British Columbia all alone?" Nuh-uh.

Bam! Two weeks later, another letter! Ugh!! I was trapped. I decided to put it off a couple of months. OK - maybe I wrote back, maybe I didn't. All I know is that at some point over a year had passed by, and the guilt was starting to pile up in my soul. Enter my brother, with a nose for guilt like a bloodhound . . .

Dave went straight for the jugular and crafted a letter from my godmother, and had it transcribed into girl-writing by his future wife. Here is what he recalls: "I can't remember exactly what was said, but it started off in the normal way: "I'm well, how are you?" The "godmother" then gradually eased into sharing some painful feelings about her loneliness, and finally ended with heart-broken accusations of betrayal by you, her godson. He then had a friend of his mail it from British Columbia, completing the subterfuge".

My wife at the time was in on the stunt, and I remember the day she came in with the mail.

"Oh - here's a letter to you from a Dorothy," she said.

An icy chill swept through my body, as the whole year of procrastination and avoidance washed over me! I was guilty and I was trapped! As I read through the letter, my worst fears were confirmed - I had broken her heart!

I recall rolling around on the couch, trying to hide under some pillows, and wishing the whole thing would just go away.

When I wrote this, I couldn't remember whether my ex-wife cracked, or my brother's smirking face gave it away, but when I finally realized I had been pranked, I was impressed[†]. Never had I realized the power of the letter. WOW!

[†] I actually just found the letter (see Figure 5.3) and the last line clearly gives it away . . .

March 19, 1991

Dear Paul,

I'm sure you're surprised to get a letter from me! Your parents gave me your new address in their last letter, so I thought I'd write to see how my "God-son" is doing! How is your job going. Last time we saw each other, you were in electrical engineering or some such confusing field. Lots of money I bet!

I don't suppose you remember what I do? That's alright, it probably wouldn't interest you anyhow. I can still remember when you were a baby — I was so proud to be your God-mother, and when you said you would write, it filled my heart with joy. But that was years ago...

Why couldn't you have been more like your brother David? Please write soon.

Your God-mother,

Dorothy R▮

Figure 5.3 **My "Godmother's" letter**

Story #60: Parental Leave

Around 2004, my brother's wife became pregnant with their third child. She worked at home running a day-care for children, and around this time the Canadian government passed a law allowing either parent to take one year of parental leave to care for the newborn child. Given their situation, my brother promptly applied for parental leave.

Initially my Dad and I were just disgusted with this situation, as it seemed like he somehow managed to scam a year vacation - which when you look at it is pretty much what he did. But what really galled us was that he proceeded to rub our faces in his good fortune at every possible opportunity. Whenever we talked to him, it was always "Hey guys! How was work today? I hope you enjoyed it." Sometimes he called me at work in the afternoon from a bar, just to really drive it home: "Hey Paul! I'm at a bar, where are you?" It was infuriating.

One night, talking with my father, we decided it was time to put a stop to this farce - but how? All sorts of crazy ideas were floated, but nothing was practical. All we knew was that it had to be some kind of letter, something that would drive an icy dagger of fear into his gloating heart. Then it hit me! The only reason that his delinquency was enabled was that his wife ran a day-care from their home, and it was solely because of this was he afforded his outrageous one year vacation.

I immediately set to work trying to find some way to connect the dots. Around this time the Canadian government had revised the Employment Insurance Act which governed how parental leave worked, as well as social insurance (equivalent to social security in the United States). Fortunately, the entire legislation was online, and

I was able to dig through it - looking for some clause that I could use to deny his parental leave. After a couple of hours of reading, I found something close enough to reference and the plan was set in motion. All I needed was Dave's social insurance number, and I knew what to do. Unfortunately, this was not that easily done. It wasn't like I could casually extract his social insurance number from him in conversation. I suspected that my father had the number in his tax return files, which stretched in an unbroken line back into the 1950's, as he claimed us both as dependents. However when I asked him to get me the number, he suddenly became reticent, and thought that maybe my prank was too extreme. I told him to think about it, and whatever he did, to not breathe a word of this to Mom, as she would immediately feel sorry for Dave and warn him.

A few days later, after another obnoxious interaction with Dave, my father forked over my brother's social insurance number and the plan was set in motion. I crafted a letter from a Pierre Durchance[†] at Human Resources and Skills Development Canada (a fancy name for the welfare and unemployment insurance administration[‡]) essentially telling my brother that his application for parental leave was denied since his wife had a stay-at-home occupation, and that he had to pay everything back. I told him in the letter that he could pay it at a nearby unemployment insurance office, or sensing he would attempt to appeal, enclosed some appeal forms, along with some official-looking tax form showing what he owed. I figured that in the worst case scenario, should he actually show up at the unemployment insurance office zoo and attempt to

[†] Durchance is French for "Hard Luck"

[‡] Humorously, in Canada unemployment insurance is nicknamed "pogey" - as in "I worked 3 months, and then went on the pogey over Christmas"

write them a check for $34,137.69, they would have no idea what to do, so he was probably safe. Lastly, I created an official-looking envelope and sent it to a friend to be mailed from eastern Canada for an official post-mark.

The following pictures are what was sent:

When Dave received it, he opened it prior to eating supper. He said that it was the driest supper he had ever eaten, as his mouth had no saliva. All he could think of was:

1) How can I pay back the money? I have to withdraw money from my RRSP (equivalent of 401K in US)

2) I have to immediately phone my boss, cancel my parental leave and beg to come back early to work.

As soon as supper was finished, he phoned Dad with his tale of woe. After going through the entire miserable story, Dave said that Dad did not seem to exhibit the appropriate level of concern. Then Dad asked "Where did you say that letter was from?" Suddenly it dawned on Dave - Paul!!

	Human Resources and Skills Development Canada	Ressources humaines et Développement des compétences Canada

Bureau of Appeals   Bureau des Appels

Assistant   Sous-ministre
Deputy Minister   adjoint
Mr. David Fuquer
░░░░░░░░ Drive
Ottawa, Ontario
KIT ░░░

Dear Mr. Fuquer:

It is with deep regret that I wish to inform you that, upon review by our office, your request for Parental Benefits has been denied. As part of our attempt to combat fraudulent claims, we routinely review cases such as yours, where the spouse owns or operates a child care facility within the applicant's home. Pursuant to the revised Employment Insurance Act, Section 18, October 2005 "Disentitlement to Benefits" and Section 23.3.3 "Parental Benefits – Limitation" it states that high-income individuals (defined by Revenue Canada as those earning in excess $80,000/year) whose spouses are engaged in "stay-at-home" occupations such as "Homemaker", or "Home Child-Care Worker" are explicitly disallowed from receiving Parental Benefits.

Consequently, you will be required to repay the benefits which you have incorrectly received, in whole or in part within 90 days of receipt of this letter. Arrangement for payment can be made at the Ottawa East Service Centre located at:

> 2339 Ogilvie Road, Gloucester, Ontario   K1A 0J6
> Beacon Hill Shopping Centre
> Phone: (613) 990-5100
> FAX: (613) 954-0676

Should you wish to file an appeal, you must do so within 30 days. In anticipation of this, please find enclosed a copy of INS-5210 "Notice of Appeal to the Board of Referees".

Sincerely,

Pierre Durchance

7530-21-936-3382 (07-05) 40

Canada

Human Resources Development Canada

Développement des ressources humaines Canada

PROTECTED WHEN COMPLETED · A
PROTÉGÉ UNE FOIS REMPLI

Social Insurance Number - Numéro d'assurance sociale

NOTICE OF APPEAL TO THE BOARD OF REFEREES

Claimant's or Other Person's Name
Nom du/de la prestataire ou autre personne

AVIS D'APPEL DEVANT LE CONSEIL ARBITRAL

Canada Customs and Revenue Agency Business No.
No. d'entreprise attribué par l'Agence des Douanes et Revenu du Canada

FOR OFFICE USE ONLY - POUR LE BUREAU SEULEMENT

Date of Receipt of this Notice of Appeal
Date de réception de cet Avis d'appel

Employer Name - Nom de l'employeur

The information you provide on this form will be retained in Personal Information Bank entitled "E.I. Claim File" (HRDC/PPU-150). Instructions for accessing your personal information are given in the **Personal Information Index,** a copy of which is available at Human Resource Centres.

Les renseignements consignés sur ce formulaire seront versés dans le fichier de renseignements personnels intitulé «Dossier de la demande de prestations» (HRDC/PPU-150). La façon de procéder pour avoir accès aux renseignements personnels vous concernant est expliquée dans le **Répertoire des renseignements personnels**. Vous pouvez consulter cette publication dans les Centre des ressources humaines du Canada.

1. Name of Appellant – Nom de l'appelant(e)

Street Address - Adresse

City - Ville   Province   Postal Code - Code Postal

Telephone (home) - Téléphone (domicile)   (   )   –   Telephone (work) - Téléphone (travail)   (   )   –

2. What decision(s) do you wish to appeal? If you are not sure what decision(s) was (were) made, please check with the Employment Insurance information centre. Quelle(s) décision(s) voulez-vous porter en appel? Si vous n'êtes pas certain quelle(s) décision(s) ont été rendues, veuillez vérifier avec le centre d'information de l'assurance-emploi.

3. Explain in as much detail as you can why you are appealing. If possible, give the reason(s) you disagree with the decision or decisions. Attach any document you have to support your viewpoint. Add more pages if you need to.

Expliquez le plus clairement possible pourquoi vous faites appel. Si possible, expliquez pourquoi vous n'êtes pas d'accord avec la/les décisions qui ont été rendues. Joignez tout document que vous avez et qui pourraient aider votre position. Ajoutez des pages au besoin.

INS 5210 (12-03) B

Canada

4. Hearing options (choose one):/ Choix d'audience (cocher une case):

☐ I wish to attend the hearing.
Je désire être présent(e) à l'audience.

☐ I wish to have a telephone hearing.
Je désire une audience par téléphone.

Language of hearing (choose one):
Langue de l'audience (cocher une case):

☐ English
Anglais

☐ French
Français

☐ I do not wish to appear at a hearing. I understand that the Board of Referees will make a decision based on my appeal and the evidence on my file.
Je ne désire pas d'audience. Je comprends que le conseil arbitral va rendre sa décision avec la documentation que contient mon dossier.

Please indicate any days or hours you are **not available** to attend a hearing:
Veuillez indiquer s'il y a des dates ou des périodes pour lesquelles vous **n'êtes pas disponible** pour assister à l'audience:

NOTE:
I understand that if I do not speak English or French it is my responsibility to provide an interpreter at my own expense. If you have a hearing or a visual impairment, HRDC will pay for either a sign language interpreter or your docket can be sent to you in Braille-let us know.

Je comprends que si je ne parle pas le français ou l'anglais, il est de ma responsabilité de fournir les services d'un interprète à mes frais. Si vous avez une déficience auditive ou visuelle, DRHC paiera les services d'un interprète gestuel, ou votre dossier vous sera envoyé en Braille. Vous n'avez qu'à nous en informer.

5. I will be represented at my hearing.
Je serai représenté(e) à l'audience.

☐ Yes
Oui

☐ No
Non

Name of representative-Nom du réprésentant:

Telephone - Téléphone:
(   )   -

Street Address - Adresse:

NOTE: If you get someone to represent you after this form is filed, you must give HRDC written authorization to release information to that person.
Si vous retenez les services d'un représentant après que vous ayez rempli ce formulaire, vous devrez donner l'autorisation écrite à DRHC avant que les informations qui vous concernent lui soient données.

6. If the information sent with this Notice of appeal is enough to cancel the decision, I wish to withdraw my appeal.
Si l'information fournie avec cet Avis d'appel est suffisante pour annuler la décision, je désire retirer mon appel.

☐ Yes
Oui

☐ No
Non

LATE APPEAL.
If this Notice of Appeal is being filed more than 30 days after the date you received your decision, you must show special reasons to extend the appeal period. Add more pages if you need to.

Reason for your delay in filing this appeal:
Date you received the decision you are appealing: _____

APPEL EN RETARD. Si cet Avis d'Appel est déposé plus de 30 jours après la date à laquelle vous avez reçu la décision, vous devez démontrer avoir des raisons spéciales pour prolonger le délai d'appel. Ajoutez des pages au besoin.

Date à laquelle vous avez reçu la décision:
Raisons pour le retard à déposer l'appel: _____

Note: Previous cases of Employment Insurance appeals on issues similar to those on your appeal can be found on the Internet at:
www.ei-ae.gc.ca/arbitre-umpire.html

Note: Des décisions sur des appels de l'assurance-emploi portant sur des causes similaires à votre appel peuvent être consultés à l'adresse Internet suivante:
www.ei-ae.gc.ca/arbitre-umpire.html

Signature ▶

Date ▶

INS 5210 (12-03) B

Canada Revenue Agency / Agence du revenu du Canada

STATEMENT OF EMPLOYMENT INSURANCE AND OTHER BENEFITS
ÉTAT DES PRESTATIONS D'ASSURANCE-EMPLOI ET AUTRES PRESTATIONS **T4E**

Year / Année	7 Repayment rate / Taux de remboursement	14 Total benefits paid / Prestations totales versées	15 Regular and other benefits paid / Prestations régulières et autres prestations versées	17 Employment benefits & support measures paid / Prestations d'emploi et mesures de soutien versées	20 Taxable tuition assistance / Aide visant les frais de scolarité imposable	21 Non-taxable tuition assistance / Aide visant les frais de scolarité non imposable
2005	30%	$34,137.69	$34,137.69	–	–	–

22 Income tax deducted / Impôt sur le revenu retenu	23 Quebec income tax deducted / Impôt du Québec sur le revenu retenu	12 Social insurance number / Numéro d'assurance sociale
$11,543.30	–	

Other information (see the back) / Autres renseignements (voir au verso)

Box / Case	Amount / Montant	Box / Case	Amount / Montant
26	$34,137.69		

Payer's name / Nom du payeur

Attach this copy to your federal return
Joignez cette copie à votre déclaration fédérale

T4E (05)

Canada Revenue Agency / Agence du revenu du Canada

STATEMENT OF EMPLOYMENT INSURANCE AND OTHER BENEFITS
ÉTAT DES PRESTATIONS D'ASSURANCE-EMPLOI ET AUTRES PRESTATIONS **T4E**

Year / Année	7 Repayment rate / Taux de remboursement	14 Total benefits paid / Prestations totales versées	15 Regular and other benefits paid / Prestations régulières et autres prestations versées	17 Employment benefits & support measures paid / Prestations d'emploi et mesures de soutien versées	20 Taxable tuition assistance / Aide visant les frais de scolarité imposable	21 Non-taxable tuition assistance / Aide visant les frais de scolarité non imposable
2005	30%	$34,137.69	$34,137.69	–	–	–

22 Income tax deducted / Impôt sur le revenu retenu	23 Quebec income tax deducted / Impôt du Québec sur le revenu retenu	12 Social insurance number / Numéro d'assurance sociale
$11,543.30	–	

Other information (see the back) / Autres renseignements (voir au verso)

Box / Case	Amount / Montant	Box / Case	Amount / Montant
26	$34,137.69		

Payer's name / Nom du payeur

Repayment chart

Complete this repayment chart if the rate in box 7 is 30% and the amount on line 234 of your return is more than $48,750.

Amount from box 15 minus the amount from box 30 when present (if negative, enter "0")	1	
Amount from line 234 of your return minus $48,750.00 (if negative, enter "0")	2	
Amount from line 1 or 2, whichever is **less**	3	
Multiply the amount on line 3 by 30% =	4	

Enter the amount from line 4 on lines 235 and 422 of your return. However, if you also received Old Age Security benefits and the amount on line 234 of your return is more than $60,806, see line 235 in your tax guide.

Tableau de remboursement

Remplissez ce tableau de remboursement si 30 % figure à la case 7 et que le montant à la ligne 234 de votre déclaration dépasse 48 750 $.

Montant de la case 15 moins le montant de la case 30 si présent (si négatif, inscrivez « 0 »)	1	
Montant de la ligne 234 de votre déclaration moins 48 750,00 $ (si négatif, inscrivez « 0 »)	2	
Inscrivez le montant le **moins élevé** : ligne 1 ou ligne 2	3	
Multipliez le montant de la ligne 3 par 30 % =	4	

Inscrivez le montant de la ligne 4 aux lignes 235 et 422 de votre déclaration. Toutefois, si vous avez aussi reçu la pension de sécurité de la vieillesse et que le montant de la ligne 234 de votre déclaration dépasse 60 806 $, lisez votre guide d'impôt à la ligne 235.

Keep this copy for your records
Conservez cette copie dans vos dossiers

T4E (05)

Story #61: The Letter Guy

My Uncle Garry in 2010 was a cheap bachelor who lived in Saskatoon, Saskatchewan (north of North Dakota) who had a Toyota Camry with many hundreds of thousands of miles (or more specifically - kilometers) on it. The car was viewed by my Dad as a death-trap, and for years he tried to get his brother Garry to buy a new car, as any time he visited his brother from eastern Canada, he was terrified to be driven around in the wreck - to the point where he used to rent a car just to avoid having to drive with Garry. Finally, a wealthy aunt of my Uncle dies and he inherits some money, which prompts him to start looking for a new car, and he settles on a Lexus IS250C convertible. Much general celebration ensues in our family. However, just after he purchases the convertible, April Fool's rolls around and he calls my Dad announcing he's reconsidered the IS 250, and is sticking with the Camry. The joke works so well, he then decides to call me and hit me with the same thing. Unfortunately, I'm in California, and it is 6am in the morning, and the prank is significantly less funny. So less funny in fact, that I vow revenge and decide to produce a fake letter from Toyota of Canada about the warranty on his convertible being void due to the extreme cold weather - which is most of the year in Saskatoon.

To execute this properly, I need the vehicle's VIN. Fortunately, my Dad is going out to visit his brother next month, so I bring him in on the plan. He is hesitant, as he figures this is a bit cruel, as his brother tends to fly off the handle when things like this happen. After 2 days of visiting my Uncle Garry, my uncle dumps a bucket of cold water on my Dad in the shower as a joke. By that evening I have the VIN.

Sitting down at my computer with the Internet and PhotoShop at hand, I craft an authentic looking letter from

a fictitious Director of Quality Assurance, Ishihito Matsumoto who is supposedly based in the head office of Toyota Canada. I even spell my Uncle's last name wrong, just to heighten the authenticity.

Now having worked for Fujitsu for a few years, I suspect that Toyota Canada is going to have a regular North American management structure, and then some sort of shadowy, parallel Japanese management structure that the North American crowd is not going to fully comprehend. Consequently, my theory is that calling the front desk of Toyota Canada and trying to find a Lexus Canada Director of Quality Assurance named Ishihito Matsumoto is going to lead into a long wild-goose chase, with no real satisfactory conclusion.

My plan works perfectly. I send the letter (see attached) to my Uncle Garry, and he loses it[†]. He goes straight to the Lexus dealer, waving the letter around, yelling, and demanding that they remedy the situation. They are puzzled, but concerned, and take the letter promising to follow up.

Around a week later, my Uncle is torn up with worry about his car, Finally the dealer calls him back. They tell him that they suspect the letter is a hoax, as nobody is able to find this Matsumoto character. Plus there is supposedly no Lexus management within the Toyota Canada operation, and there is definitely no "Cold Weather" clause in the warranty - at least that anyone can confirm (God Bless Japanese management!).

At this point my Uncle suspects some local buddies of his, lays low and waits for his adversary to show his face. Just

[†] I had my cousin in Toronto mail it - yeah, that's right Dear Cuz - you too are now on Garry's revenge list . . .

for good measure I phone up my Uncle when he's at work, and leave a message on his answering machine from Matsumoto-san expressing condolences on the car purchase, and as compensation offering a complementary bus pass, which can be picked up at the dealer.

Eventually my Dad gives it away, as it drives him crazy that we haven't heard anything from Garry, and he has to call him. We all have a good laugh, and at the dealer they now know my Uncle as "The Letter Guy."

Toyota Motor Manufacturing Canada   February 18, 2020
1055 Fountain St. North
PO Box 5002
Cambridge, ON
N3H 5K2

Mr. Gerald Fuqer
░░░░░░ **Avenue**
Saskatoon, Saskatchewan
S7N ░░░░

Regarding: Lexus IS 250 C - VIN # JTHFF2C░░░░░░░░

Dear Mr. Fuqer,

I wish to congratulate you on your purchase of your Lexus IS 250 C. The Lexus brand of Toyota is very pleased with the acceptance of this car in Canada. Unfortunately this vehicle was not designed for such extreme winters as are experienced in Saskatchewan, and as a result the warranty is voided if this vehicle is operated below -15°C[†]. I hope that this is not too inconvenient and I wish again to congratulate you on your purchase.

Should you have any questions about your warranty, please do not hesitate to contact us at 1-800-265-3987 between 8:00am and 6:00pm Eastern Time.

Regards,

Ishihito Matsumoto
Director of Quality Assurance
Lexus Division

[†] Lexus General Warranty Clause 28.4.5.6 - Harsh / Extreme Winter Conditions

7530-21-936-3382 (07-05) 40

Story #62: Gus Is 13

Up until this point, I have not mentioned the fact that I am married to Natasha, and we have two kids named Gus and Montana who in the summer of 2016 were 11 and 9 respectively. Now we routinely tease the kids with stuff like "When the ice-cream truck plays the song, it means he's out of ice-cream" (Ray Romano's line from "Everybody Loves Raymond") and other low-grade silliness, but nothing to the level of the tales recounted in this book.

However, in 2016 prior to my son's 12th birthday on June 4, he started to annoy us with his constant excitement about the upcoming day and anticipated presents, so my wife and I came in the door with the following:

Gus: "I can't wait for my birthday tomorrow - can you tell me what you got me now?"

Paul: "What do you mean tomorrow (June 4)? You were born on the 15th. You're birthday is still a couple of weeks away"

Gus: "No it isn't! It's tomorrow"

Natasha: "No Gus - your Dad's right. You were born on the 15th, and we just always chose to celebrate your birthday on the 4th as all of your friends always went away on vacation as soon as school ended. You're old enough now to know the truth and you're just going to have to wait until your real birthday."

Gus: [growing agitated] "It is not! You guys are just teasing me!"

Paul: "How do you know? Have you ever seen your birth certificate? I'll get it and prove it to you."

Gus: "OK - go get it!"

Paul: [an idea starting to form and addressing Natasha] "Where is his birth certificate? Is it in the attic?"

Natasha: [knowing full well that his birth certificate is not in the attic] "How about you look for it tomorrow. We're trying to finish this movie and the kids have to go to bed as it is a school night."

Paul: "Good point. Gus - I'll get it tomorrow and you'll see that we aren't just making this up."

Now there are two facts involving age that are absolute certainties with kids:

1) They have no way to prove anything about when they were born, as their memories about their life grow increasingly hazy as you stretch back towards their birth.

2) The idea that they are somehow behind their peers and should have been a grade ahead in school is utter torture. If they get wind of anything that suggests this they go mental.

With this knowledge, I filled Natasha in on my scheme after the kids went to bed: next day I would go to work and create an altered version of Gus's birth certificate, leaving the day as it was correctly supposed to be: June 4, but moving the year back one from 2004 to 2003. She thought it was genius.

The next day, armed with Photoshop, I created the altered birth certificate, printed it out on the printer at home, and texted Natasha that Gus's "birth certificate" was ready. Natasha recorded the whole thing on her cell-phone, but

here is the transcript starting after Gus returns from getting his "birth-certificate" from the printer:

Natasha: "What Gus? I don't understand."

Gus: "Date of birth! 6-4-2003!!"

Natasha: "So?"

Gus: [in a hysterical high-pitched voice] "I'm 12 years old!!!!"

Natasha: [starting to laugh, and trying to control it] "What? What?"

Gus: [with continuing hysteria] "I'M 12 YEARS OLD!!! I"M GOING TO TURN 13!!!!"

Natasha: [still laughing] "Oh my God . . ."

Gus: [still hysterical] "I'm turning 13 you f. (Gus controls himself and refrains from swearing). My GOD!!! [Gus starts to cry]. Oh my God - I thought I was a year younger my whole life! I'm going to be 13 [sobbing]

Natasha: [continuing to chuckle, and offering somewhat helpfully] "You should be in the next grade then."

Gus: "Two grades."[†]

Natasha: [starts to really laugh again]

[†] Gus did kindergarten twice - once in Russian and once in Spanish immersion, so technically this would have been two grades, but because of his birthday, it was optional when he started kindergarten.

Gus: "Oh my God!"

Natasha: "You should be in, ah, what grade then? You should be in middle school now!"

Gus: [still hysterical] "I know!!! [sobbing] Oh my God! Oh my God! I've got to tell my friends! [more sobbing]"

Natasha: "How did we miss the whole year?"

Gus: [still hysterical but growing angry] "I don't friggin' know!!! [sobs some more and runs upstairs to tell his sister].

Montana!! Your brother is turning 13 years old. [sob] Oh my God!"

Natasha: [now serious] "Montana. It looks like Gus is turning 13.

Gus: [continuing hysterical] "I'm going to be a teenager tomorrow!"

Natasha: "I know. We thought he was born in 2004, but he was born in 2003."

Natasha: "How did we miss the whole year?"

Montana: [incredulous] "What? Are you serious?"

Natasha: "Yeah! We just saw it"

Montana: "What? No way!"

Natasha: "He should be in the next grade. He should be in middle school now."

Montana: "Oh my God! We have to tell everyone! [pause] We have to tell the principal"

Natasha: "Tell the principal? Then what? He skips another . . . He can't skip a grade."

Montana: "Gus is turning 13 tomorrow!"

Gus: "I can go home by myself already!"

Montana: [starting to cry] "Gus!"

Gus: "I know! I thought I was 11 years old my whole life. I thought I was 11 years old . . ."

Natasha: "Sorry Gus . . ."

At this point things degenerated with Montana starting to cry because she didn't want her brother to be a teenager because they were terrible, and Gus started to relate the story of total delinquency on the part of his parents to his friends.

Later that afternoon, we told him the truth. He didn't think it was a very funny joke, but we did. However, as he started to relate the story to his friends, and they laughed, the appreciation factor went up. I know he'll pay us back for this some day.

Story #63: The Doctor's Appointment

Now this is one of the all-time great practical jokes, and it's brilliance is it's sheer simplicity, and the credit for this one entirely belongs to Dave.

So my Mom and Dad are old-school and don't use things like Outlook or cell-phones, and run the scheduling in their

life with a paper calendar, marking things like Doctor's appointments onto the appropriate day in ink with a pen.

This calendar also held a strange fascination for my brother who seemed to enjoy marking unusual things in it, like Hitler's birthday, the fall of Saigon, etc. It was sort of like a weird version of Google's splash page, filled with bizarre events and birthdays. The discovery of one of my brother's notations always caused some minor "Ha, ha" from Mom, but pretty much everyone else just accepted this as a quirk of Dave's personality and essentially ignored it.

About 6 or 7 years ago, my brother, who now is married with kids, but still frequents Mom and Dad's house because of food and laundry benefits (and still marks up the calendar for no good reason), gets the idea of marking in a note a couple of months in the future saying: "Doctor's Appt 11:00am," in a print that is sort of an amalgam of both their styles. Now my parents routinely bicker like an old married couple (surprise - they are one), and at some point, one of them notices this "Doctor's Appointment" note, which specifies a time, but no details about which doctor. Since they both had multiple doctors that this could refer to, the recriminations immediately start. Mom accuses Dad of writing this note, and Dad fiercely denies it, instead blaming her for being dopey and not writing the details herself. Fortunately the appointment is still several weeks away, so they start calling all of the doctors they can think of. Nothing - no record of anything. The date creeps closer, and panic starts as they realize they are going to get charged for a no-show. The recriminations become more intense, and they are at each other's throats. Finally one of them closely examines the hand-writing, and the skulduggery is revealed. That mutt David!

Suddenly, the sword of Damocles is withdrawn and relief floods their souls. They are not going to embarrass themselves with a shameful no-show, and even better, are not going to pay for a service not rendered. Life is good, and general hilarity ensues with the recounting of the tale to their friends.

Story #64: The Phantom Buyer

Here is another one that my nasty piece-of-work brother pulled on my poor dear Mom. I vaguely recall hearing about this, but it was after I had left home, so I didn't have ringside seats for the aftermath, and it was only after I ran this whole collection of stupidity by my brother that he reminded me of this.

At some point in the late 1970's or early 1980's my Mom decided that if she didn't escape from home, she would go crazy. Consequently she decided to become a real-estate agent. After getting her license, she would spend weekends running open-houses, and routinely be gone during the week showing houses.

One day when my brother was in university, he decided to leave a note for my mom. Here is how he tells it:

"For some reason, I felt the same desire to prank Mom that you did. So one day I left her a note by the back door, explaining that someone called and was very interested in one of the houses she had listed. "Please call [I gave some random first name] as soon as you get in." My writing wasn't the best to begin with, and I made sure the bogus number I wrote was completely illegible. I erased it multiple times, and may have left a number out, just to be sure. I got home later, having forgotten about the note, to find a frantic Mom wondering what the number was."

Nice . . .

Story #65: Dave Buys A House

OK - so this isn't really a "written word" story, but it seems to fit nicely here, so here goes: After graduating university, my brother got a good government job, and proceeded to stash away all of his earnings, whilst comfortably living at home with Mom and Dad. My Mom (who had gotten her real-estate license as per the previous story) started to get concerned that Dave was never going to move out. He used to "joke" with my parents about "when we retire together", but my Mom was starting to get concerned that it actually wasn't a joke.

She started looking for a small condominium for him, but regardless of what she found, he seemed uninterested. Finally she approached me and asked if I thought Dave was serious about buying a house.

"Serious?" I snorted. "Dave is never going to leave - period. The only way you'll pry him out is if you find a house and make him sign the offer and the down-payment check. Otherwise - happy retirement with Dave and Dad".

After a few more months, my Mom finally agreed with me and made Dave buy a house. I took a picture of him rolling around on the couch, trying to hide his head under a pillow, while Mom holds a clipboard with the offer and a pen, but I couldn't find it. I wish I could - it was hilarious.

As a footnote to the story, his condo became what I called "the clubhouse", as the only thing he did there was sleep and play video games with his loser friends. He still came back for supper every night at my parents, along with his laundry on the weekend. Then he got a girlfriend, and suddenly the house wasn't such a bad idea . . .

Story #66: An Unused Typewriter

This next story also comes from my brother, even though I was apparently a part of it, and involves a friend of my brother named Eric A. Apparently my parents at some point purchased an IBM Selectric typewriter (frankly I don't recall this at all, as all I remember is some old Smith-Corona dog of a manual typewriter that I used to bang my high-school assignments out on - see the next story for details) and Eric wanted to borrow it. Here are my brother's words:

"*Speaking of Eric, I can't recall the exact details, but I think Mom and Dad were on vacation in Egypt. So it was just you and me . . . On a Saturday Eric asked if he could borrow our high-tech electric (ball) typewriter. We said sure. Then for some reason, we had to step out. Not knowing if we'd miss Eric, we decided to leave the typewriter out for him. It was clearly visible through the back door window, sitting on the kitchen table with paper in it. We kindly left a note taped to the inside of the door, telling him to let himself in . . . with the key that was also taped to the inside of the door.*

I don't know why we found that so funny, but it was. Eric was not able to share our laughter."

Frankly Dave was a real dick. There is no way I would have done such a cruel thing - it must have been all him. Yeah right . . .

Story #67: The "Skipmaster 2000"

As I alluded in the previous story, we used to have an old Smith-Corona manual typewriter of the same vintage as the one Moses used to type out the Ten Commandments. The thing was a pain-in-the-butt, and I remember my inability to hit the "a" key hard enough with my left little pinky finger to actually type an "a" - a particularly annoying

feature. Another aspect of this baby was that if you didn't adroitly strike a key and withdraw your finger, the hammer would strike the letter, but would then bounce back on the still depressed key and hammer an offset ghost of the letter, as the carriage had started advancing on the second impact. This effect I would use to torture high-school teachers I disliked.

By Grade 12 I had become a good enough typist to either deliver a cleanly typed assignment, or an assignment that looked like an astigmatism simulation with one clear set of print, and then a slightly offset ghost of the same thing, lurking up and to the right. Reading one of these gave you a headache after a few pages, and only by continuously looking away from the page could you avoid getting sick. Teachers I liked got a clean version, and teachers I disliked got the vomit-inducing version. A typical conversation went like this:

> **Teacher:** "Paul - you have to retype this assignment. I can't read it."

> **Paul:** "I've tried several times sir. It's the typewriter - there's something wrong with it"

> **Teacher:** "Can't your parents get it fixed, or can't you borrow another one from a friend."

> **Paul:** "No sir - we don't have the money, and I don't know anybody else with a typewriter. They all come to use ours."

What a load of crap. But it worked - they eventually just accepted that they had to suffer through reading my assignments this way. I'm sure this "benefitted" my grades, but I was too stupid enjoying my revenge to look at the big

picture. Plus I probably wound up increasing the revenues for our local optometry community.

5.4 Work Adventures

This section details some humorous episodes of pranks from work, and many are from my brother who worked for the Canadian government.

Story #68: The Herman-Miller Chair

At one point in my career, I sat in a cubicle next to a nice, but somewhat whiney software engineer named Paul B - sort of a technical version of Ray Romano. This guy had permanent back issues, and hated the chair that he was assigned - the standard 5-wheel office chair. He complained endlessly about it, and was locked in a death-grip with HR[†] to get him a "proper" Herman-Miller chair with the appropriate lumbar support. In the interim, he attempted to modify his current chair with lumbar pillows and those mats made out of wooden balls that taxi drivers seem to like. Nothing worked. Finally after months of complaining, our department head signed off on getting him an orthopedic assessment, and the ticket to his dream chair was within his grasp.

After the assessment, he finally was allowed to order his precious chair, and the waiting game began. One month passed - no chair. The people in HR had long-ago lost all respect for him, and seemed to actually enjoy his childish impatience. Two months passed - with lots more complaining and futile attempts to ascertain the chair's whereabouts - all to no avail. Finally, after about three months, the magic day arrived and the Herman-Miller "Wonder-Chair" appeared in all it's glory, wrapped in

---

† Human-resources

packing cellophane. As fate would have it, Paul B was absent - but I was there in the next cube.

It took only a few minutes of staring at this plastic-covered beauty before I knew what had to be done. Not knowing when Paul was coming back, I grabbed the closest accomplice, and we set about unwrapping his new chair, and then wrapping up his old chair in the same material. Fortunately, the God of Pranks smiled on us, and we were able to complete our task before Paul came back from whatever software engineers do in the afternoon.

The effect was everything we hoped for. As soon as Paul B saw the cellophane covered chair sitting in his cube, a little squeal of joy escaped his lips followed by "Finally! It's here!!" He sprinted the last few feet and started unwrapping the chair. We had to leave as we were starting to lose it, and couldn't keep a straight face.

From the vantage point of my next-door cube, we listened as the final pieces of cellophane were pulled off and the confusion and anger set it in.

"What the hell!!? God-damnit! I can't believe it!", Paul spluttered turning red with anger.

"What's wrong?" I asked, barely holding it together enough to sound innocently curious.

"Those idiots ordered me the wrong chair. It's the same chair I used to have!" he panted. In fact, it was the exact same chair he used to have.

At this point we lost it, and started roaring with laughter, tears streaming down our cheeks. However, he didn't realize that it was a prank, and thought we were just laughing at his misfortune - something he was apparently

well acquainted with. Realizing he hadn't clued in yet, I decided to keep pushing it.

"Are you sure it isn't a different chair?" I asked innocently. "Maybe they changed the model?"

"No!" he yelled. "Look it even has the same fabric as my old chair. In fact...."

At this point, the realization dawned on him that it was in fact his old chair, and he realized his "concerned" office mates were in fact the evil hand behind this grim twist of fate.

At this point we wheeled in the Herman-Miller "Wonder-Chair" from the next cube, and all was suddenly right with the world.

Story #69: Desk Phones

Back in the day before cell-phones, people relied on their desk phones for communication, which afforded all sorts of prank material.

1) Disconnect or just plain remove the cord from the receiver to the phone base. A dash to the desk to answer a ringing phone would find you holding a receiver in your hand with the cord either missing or dangling from it.

2) Remove the microphone. This was always fun as the person would grow increasingly loud trying to make the person at the far-end hear them.

3) Honey on the earpiece. This speaks for itself.

Story #70: Black Cardboard

One time my brother's coworkers removed the mouthpiece plastic and taped thick cardboard over the microphone, essentially muffling anything my brother said into the phone, making it very difficult for the person on the far end to hear anything. They then proceeded to enjoy a week of my brother shouting into the phone to try and do his job.

Story #71: The Shy Bladder - 3 Short Stories

At my brother's work, Dave discovered that one of his colleagues was basically unable to piss when anyone was present in the bathroom (Canadian for restroom). He would wait until non-peak times and then head off into the far corners of their building to be able to have a stall in an abandoned bathroom. Once my brother became attuned to his colleague's issue, he began to follow him to the bathroom, and verifying it was the proper victim via the shoe-check, he swung into action.

1) His initial attacks involved an "Uncle Ted - The Guy Who Wouldn't Leave" strategy[†]. Dave would walk in and proceed to noisily screw around at the sink, whistling, rinsing his mouth, cleaning the counter, combing his hair, and generally just preventing his colleague from pissing. Then he'd eventually just sit on the counter and wait. Finally after a painfully long time, he'd ask "Stefan - are you OK in there?" which would prompt some cursing when his colleague realized what was being done to him.

2) Phase 2 of the strategy involved waiting until Stefan was in the stall and then Dave would come running into the bathroom with a mouth full of water and after kicking

---

[†] I have no idea from where in my brother's twisted mind he came up with "Uncle Ted" as there is no Ted of any sort in our family.

open the neighboring stall, proceed to simulate somebody vomiting.

3) Phase 3, which was most genius, was coming to the neighboring stall with a glass of water, unzipping his pants, and simulating pissing standing up. Then at the end, Dave trailed the "stream of piss" over the edge of the toilet and onto the floor, heading towards Stefan's shoes, generating more cursing from Stefan.

Story #72: The Conference

One time at my brother's work, they had to send a representative to a conference that nobody wanted to attend. Eventually they managed to convince one of their co-workers (Anna) to attend, but only on the condition that she would only be an observer and not have to give any presentations. With this setup, my brother promptly intercepted the real agenda and replaced it with a doctored version. He typed it up on paper, misspelling his colleague's name, faxed it a couple of times to himself, set a mug of coffee on it, and then put it on her desk. The agenda now had the following features:

1) The conference went from 6am to 7pm every day, with a 30 minute lunch break to allow the attendees to run out and buy a lunch

2) Monday afternoon Anna was scheduled to talk for 6 hours, with a 3 hour follow-up session on Tuesday morning.

3) The conference ended on Friday for all at noon, except for several key participants - which obviously included Anna.

She was not happy.

5.5 Air Travel

Here are three short stories about air travel that I hope you will find amusing:

Story #73: Dave and Flying

Dave has always been afraid of flying, and consequently I found it amusing to sit beside him on plane flights to talk about wing stress issues and aluminum fatigue - especially during turbulence. One time prior to going on a long flight to Germany, I printed off an article on plane crashes, and how the largest percentage of crashes occurred during take-off. I then handed this article to my brother just as we were taxiing to the runway. Dave greatly enjoyed how I helped enrich his life.

Story #74: Mogadishu

In my company, one of the guys who used to be in my group was very paranoid about flying, and continuously studied all plane-crash statistics, as well as airline and airplane safety records. You could ask him about any airplane, and he could immediately tell you its safety record, including how many crashes and incidents it had. He was a walking NTSB journal and Soviet era aircraft terrified him the most. Based on these deep-seated fears of his, I waited for the day he would have to travel. Finally we had to go to Israel, and knowing his fears, I created a nightmare itinerary flying Air Nigeria connecting through Mogadishu to Tel Aviv, and told him that we had to fly this route as it was the cheapest. Just for extra spice, I told him Air Nigeria was still flying Tu-144s. He knew off the top of his head that there were 16 built and 2 crashed.

Story #75: Returning A Gift

One time, some friends of ours in Chicago lent us their RV for a couple of weeks. In exchange for the favor, we

promised to buy them tickets to see us in California. However, after some thought, we cranked out the worst possible itinerary, and sent it to them proudly. It had them departing Chicago Midway at 5:35am and making a couple of 3 hour connections in various cities around America, and finally arriving 13 hours later into SFO. It produced the desired effect of outrage in our friends when they realized the nightmare travel they were now signed up for.

5.6 Hallowe'en

This section discusses a couple of humorous Hallowe'en related episodes.

Story #76: The Ghost In The Basement

For some strange reason my Mom owned an old black-velvet opera "cape" that easily could have been worn by a Dementor around Hogwarts. We used to put it on and try and scare each other by coming out of closets at night in the thing. We even perfected it by making two glow-in-the-dark plastic "eyes" from an old "glow-in-the-dark" key-chain,[†] but after a while it got pretty lame. That is until one of my brother's friends (George M - a son of Greek immigrants) came over and we pulled this stunt on him. He freaked and ran screaming out of the house. I don't know what sorts of night terrors lurk in the Greek mind, but man, did they ever respond well to this. After he settled down, and we got him to come back inside the house, he decided that this was exactly what his younger sister needed.

One winter day, when it got dark early, we went over to George's place after school and before his sister got home[‡]. She knew Dave, and having Dave hanging around

---

[†] You know - the kind of plastic that glows green after exposure to bright light.

with George was not unusual so they were the straight-men in the setup. As his sister had never seen me before, I went down into the basement, and dressed in the Dementor robe, with green cat-eyes taped to my cheeks, and a long bicycle chain[†] for appropriate effect. I had a flashlight to pump up the glowing eyes, and George showed me where the main power switch on the breaker panel was. Then we proceeded to wait for his sister to arrive.

After her arrival, we gave her about 15 minutes to head to her room before I killed the power.

George's Sister: [emerging from her room sort of scared] "What happened? Why are the lights out?"

George: "Ah - it's just a power failure."

Dave: "Yeah - this kind of thing happens a lot in the winter."

[George's sister is not really buying it, and is very nervous. Then I rattle a chain in the basement, and she freaks.]

George's Sister: [screams] "What's that noise?? Oh my God!"

George: "Hear what? I didn't hear anything."

Dave: "Neither did I."

[I rattle the chain again and start to head up the basement stairs, which are straight down from the front

---

[‡] His parents ran a restaurant, so they got home late.

[†] Ghosts apparently always drag chains around.

door, and separated from the hallway by a railing so that you could see someone coming up.]

George's Sister: [screams louder] "There it is again! It's in the basement! We have to get out of here!"

[At this point it is totally obvious that she is not "hearing things" as I am slowly clomping up the stairs, dragging the chain. Meanwhile Dave and George have placed themselves in the front entry-way of George's house, where they are fumbling with their boots, and blocking the front door.]

George's Sister: [panicking and becoming really hysterical] "Get out! Get out! Please let me out!"

George: "I am. I just have to get my boots on. It's cold out. Do you want your jacket?"

[I emerge from the basement in my robe and she sees the glowing eyes and totally panics. Screaming and crying, she claws her way past George and Dave and runs out into the snow in her socks]

It took her about 15 minutes to be able to breathe normally, and after she finally settled down enough to be able to look at me in the costume, her first thought was to do this to her friend.

Story #77: Frozen Vegetables

A quick note. On Hallowe'en, get an old frozen-vegetable bag, or even an onion bag, and put the candy in there. The expression on the children's faces as you reach into the bag for "vegetables" is priceless, and parents think it is funny.

Story #78: The Gargoyle

About 4 years ago we upped the ante. Natasha got a gargoyle body suit as a Hallowe'en costume (see Figure 5.4). Around this time, Gus decided he was too big to go trick-or-treating, and instead wanted to scare kids. We bought a fog machine, got strobe lights, put on the Hallowe'en channel on Pandora, and tied a string to the front door so it would "open on it's own."[†] Wrapped in a black sheet with corpse makeup, I would distribute "vegetables" or this year "onions," while Natasha would crouch at the end of the sidewalk by the street where the parents waited. They would all think she was a plastic Hallowe'en decoration, until she stood up. The result was parents jumping back, screaming - with some even running into the street for safety. It was awesome!

[†] Apparently a form of high magic to most kids in our neighborhood - including the teenagers. Seriously - I answer more questions every year from astounded kids about "How did the door open on its own?"

Figure 5.4 **The gargoyle**

5.7 The Future

Since nothing has really changed, there is always something new cooking.

Story #79: The Playboy Subscription

As I write this, I am visiting my Uncle Garry[†]. Yesterday as we laughed about some of these stories, we began to think of things we could do to my Dad. The key to psychologically torturing my father is to create something that will either appear to ruin the perfection of his house, or cause apparent personal embarrassment to him. We settled on the latter.

The initial suggestion was to have some mail-order cannabis sent to him at Christmas while my Uncle was visiting. Since cannabis is now legal in Canada, you can actually mail-order it. The idea of some ganja showing up with Edwin's name on it, and my Uncle's shocked and disapproving look as he said something like "Edwin! I can't believe that you are into marijuana!" would have been priceless.

While this would have produced the appropriate responses in my father: disbelief, turning red, denial, etc. it would have required the package to physically show up when my Uncle was visiting, as well as him being present to intercept the delivery. At this point my Uncle suggested a genius plan: get my father a gift subscription to Playboy Magazine. This was truly genius, as it would repeatedly show up throughout the year, and would result in my father being forced to hide from the mailman for the next several years, knowing that the mailman knew that Edwin subscribed to Playboy Magazine. The mere appearance of the mailman would inevitably send my father scurrying

[†] My Dad's younger brother, and "The Letter Guy"

inside, to hide until he left. The problem was that if I just got him the gift subscription, he would immediately know where it came from. Fortunately, the Playboy website allows the owner of the credit card to be different than the one paying for the gift. This was perfect as my parents have friends who could technically be capable of pulling such a stunt. My Uncle and I decided that we would have the gift be from another friend of my parents - a certain Terry H. This would result in my father quietly confronting Terry, and Terry denying any knowledge of the prank - something my father would not believe at all. After all of the inquiries and recriminations were past, the assumption is that they would then look for a 3rd party in their circle of friends who would be capable of setting them both up. In our opinion, this would be another character named Jim L. We figured this would take several weeks to sort out, in order to convince those involved that none of them was lying, and only after that would my Dad's eyes begin to cast further afield, and eventually he would come up with me. Of course I plan on blaming his brother Garry.

June 6: I bought the gift subscription yesterday afternoon.

August 26: No news. Garry and I are trying to come up with a way of smoking him out, without immediately making it clear who was involved. No ideas yet.

October 5: I finally get my Mom on the phone without my Dad (neither of them have a cell phone) and confess to what we have done, and then enlist her help to drive the prank home. She is enthusiastic and together we come up with the idea of her discussing with my brother during Canadian Thanksgiving supper how they've gotten this Playboy magazine subscription and they can't figure out where it's from. Then Dave will say that he just read that a Canadian feminist hacker just published all the name of

Playboy subscribers in Canada online. Edwin will then turn white, the prank will end, and humor will ensue.

Next I write an e-mail to my brother, explaining the plan:

From: Paul Fuquer

Sent: Saturday, October 05, 2019 12:38 PM

To: 'David Fuquer'

Subject: Need your help

Dave,

I need your help finishing off a practical joke. When Gus and I went to see Garry, Garry and I got the brilliant idea of getting Dad a subscription to Playboy. I did it as a gift from Terry H to slow Dad down if he immediately suspected me. The idea was that if this thing showed up in the mail, he would be horrified. Then he would realize that the mailman would know what the magazine was in the brown wrapper, and at that point Dad would never be able to greet the mailman again – knowing that he knew Dad's secret. So all great and everything – except we haven't heard a word. Garry and I have been wracking our brains on how to "smoke him out", but up until now nothing.

This morning I talked with Mom by herself and finally confessed to her what we had done. She then said that she remembered one showing up (they went to 4x per year print edition), but didn't know what happened to it. After a few minutes of thinking about how to drive it home, the idea of how to solve the Gordian knot came to me, and here is where you come in.

Next time you are at dinner at their place, Mom is going to bring up how "the weirdest thing happened – a Playboy magazine addressed to Edwin Fuquer showed up". At this point (and feel free to improvise as you see fit), you get concerned and remember reading a few weeks ago how a militant feminist hacker hacked into the Playboy website and published the names and addresses of all Playboy subscribers in Canada. After you play Dad for as long as possible (or you lose it ☺), Mom is going to ask "BTW Ed – what did you do with that Playboy magazine?". I give it an 80% + chance that he didn't just stick it in the recycle, and that he turns beet red before stuttering out some sort of "I threw it out!".

Anyway – Mom is queued up, so just rehearse her two lines with her prior to dinner so that you get the appropriate setup.

Enjoy, and let me know how it goes down,

P

P.S. I told Garry that I'd blame the whole thing on him ☺

And that was it. Canadian Thanksgiving came and went. Several more days go by - nothing. At the end of the week, I ask Dave what's up, and he says "Nothing - the subject never came up". Yeah - right.

About a month later, I got Mom on the phone again by herself, and asked her what happened. She said that she forgot, and after "remembering" said "Your Dad cancelled the subscription". What a load of crap.

Two weeks ago, Garry went to visit my Dad, and I told him the whole thing stunk, and that they were just jacking with us. I suggested that at this point there was no way to "smoke them out" and that the best thing was to just take it head on and at supper say "So Edwin - what's up with your Playboy subscription?". That was a week ago, and nothing from him either. I guess the chickens have come home to roost.

Story #80: The Folded Twenty

My daughter likes to keep a folded $20 bill in her clear plastic cell phone protector "in case of emergencies"[†].

[†] Apparently the sort of emergencies we are talking about is having to buy more popcorn at a movie, or having to buy some candy at the 7-11.

Figure 5.5 **My daughter's phone**[1]
1. If you, the astute reader, are wondering why there is a ruler in the picture, it was to properly scale the photograph I took prior to printing a fake one.

One day, whilst looking at this folded bill, it occurred to me that it would be almost impossible to notice the difference between the real folded $20 bill, and a properly trimmed photocopy of the folded bill (one-sided of course!)

This prank has a slow-burning fuse, but at some point she'll want to buy some candy and find that the $20 bill is only a one-sided picture.

By the way - my daughter has been harassing me for over a year to put a lock on her bedroom to "keep her evil brother out". After teasing them both that I'd install locking door knobs on their rooms, but threatening to have them keyed the same, I finally installed the locking door knobs,

Figure 5.6 **The fake $20**

but put Montana's backwards, so that the lock is on the inside!. I'll keep you posted as to the results in a future book.

Figure 5.7 **Bedroom door lock**

Appendix A: The Reserves

I am writing this appendix to describe some stories from my time in the Canadian Artillery Reserves.

Story #81: Air Cadets

Being a typical teenage boy, I had been raised on war-movies, toy guns, and model tanks and wanted action - now! Boy-Scouts didn't cut it, but my friend Sandy had joined something called Air-Cadets

Apparently if you joined, and then signed up for some special training, you could fly jets in the summer, or something like that. Whatever - it was better than Boy Scouts, and related to the military. I signed up immediately.

After getting the uniform and boots, I soon found that it was not exactly how I imagined it. Only if you put a pile of time into it, and went through a bunch of training programs, could you maybe, just maybe, get to go to an Air Force base. In the meantime, there were boots to polish, and drill moves to be learned - in fact lots of drill moves, and lots of polishing. More so than Sandy and I cared for. Soon, we'd show up for assembly, get counted, and then jump out the window when the sergeant wasn't looking and go hang out until Sandy's Dad picked us up. Why didn't we just quit? Who knows? Maybe we were worried about getting yelled at by Sandy's Dad who drove us and was a somewhat scary guy.

Story #82: The 30th Field Artillery

One night at air-cadets Sandy announced that he had found something infinitely better than our current situation: Militia. Or more properly, The Reserves. It was like

The "Letter Guy" and Other Stories

air-cadets, but more real - and you got paid!! All you needed to join was to be 17 - something I wasn't for another 9 months.

Sandy immediately quit, and lacking an alternative ride to air-cadets, so did I. Unfortunately Sandy joined a Service Division reserve which basically fixed vehicles, and was not for me. However, digging around in the phone book, and asking various people, it appeared that there was an artillery reserve in Ottawa. Yeah Baby! Blowing things up with large caliber guns - that was my dream!

I counted down the days until my 17th birthday, and the week after I enrolled. Thus began my 4 year journey towards total disenchantment with anything military. I'll skip the standard stories about being yelled at in basic training, etc. and move straight to some of the more humourous stories.

Story #83: Equipment

The Canadian reserves are the lowest rung on the Canadian military ladder. Consequently, we got the worst equipment. Sleeping bags smelled and had holes. Air mattresses leaked, leaving you on the ground in the morning. Winter equipment was never sufficient for the conditions you faced. I remember one freezing night, huddled under some artillery crates on frozen ground at 2am, trying to stay warm in a canvas fall jacket. It was insane. (It was during this particular night that I learned that the worst times make the best stories). Next morning, when they brought the kitchen trucks by with food, we would take hard-boiled eggs and put them in our pockets just to try and warm up.

Story #84: Exercises

Once a month, we'd go on exercises for the weekend. We departed Friday night and returned Sunday evening. For new recruits, these were torture, as you basically got no sleep, and were doing guard duty in the middle of the night, typically in the rain or snow (it was always muddy), and just generally miserable. Most of the time we'd go to Petawawa, (the swamp and mosquito infested forest north-west of Ottawa that I mentioned in Story #55), but sometimes to Fort Drum in New York. Before you left, you were issued a weapon, blank ammunition, and a blank-firing attachment - which was something you stuck on the end of the rifle or machine-gun to get the appropriate blow-back to operate the gas recoil mechanism.

I remember the first time I finally got to fire my Sterling sub-machine gun (SMG) during exercises. I had two 30-round magazines full of 9 mm blanks, and as soon as I was attacked, "Brrrapp", "Brra - ", click, click, click. I couldn't believe it - 30 rounds gone in a heartbeat. So much for everything I'd been taught in war movies.

Worse - once you fired it, the blanks fouled everything and resulted in hours of cleaning once you got back to base. You weren't allowed to leave until your weapon was cleaned. Ugh! Finally, I learned that the seasoned members of our regiment brought along an oily paper towel, and when heading out on exercise, stuffed it down the barrel, put the breach-block in their pocket, and threw away the ammunition. This resulted in a perfectly clean weapon, and a quick departure[†].

[†] Not too quick, or you'd be busted. It wasn't like the sergeants didn't know these tricks.

Story #85: The Night Attack

One time during a winter exercise (it always seemed to be winter), some of the sergeants and master corporals (Master Bombadiers in the British system) attacked our gun-emplacement in the middle of the night. It was cold, we were dead tired, and this was the last thing we wanted to see. Our sergeant pulled open the tent, and kicking sleeping bags said "Everybody out! We're being attacked!" Ugh!! We burrowed deeper into our sleeping bags. The poor bastards by the door sustained multiple kicks to the ribs until they finally cracked and got out, but if you slept at the very back, you could usually dodge having to get out. Finally the sergeant went away, and the "attack" commenced. I still remember one time looking safely through the flap of my tent at the neighbouring tent, where a machine gunner had just stuck his C2[†] out the tent flap, and was just proceeding to burn off his ammunition in long continuous bursts at nothing.

Story #86: Heading Out On Exercise

Once you became a Bombadier (Corporal) in the artillery, life was about as good as it got. You had minimal responsibility, but were also an accepted member of the unit, so you got to dodge a lot of crap. You were also fully "on the inside", so things that were forbidden to privates and new recruits, were now afforded to you. For instance, when we headed out on exercise, we typically took lots of alcohol. Beer was stuffed under the cabs of our two and a half ton trucks[‡], and bottles of liquor placed down the barrels of our 105mm guns, cushioned by rolls of toilet paper. You could also bring your own air-mattress -

---

[†] Fully automatic version of the Belgian FN 7.26mm

[‡] Deuce and a halfs" or just plain "deuces"

regardless of how ridiculous it looked. For instance I had a stripey orange-and-brown one.

On one particular weekend when we were heading up to Petawawa, one of the sergeants was drinking a beer while driving and got pulled over by the highway patrol. They were in the process of ripping apart his vehicle, when my part of the convoy arrived and witnessed what was happening. We laughed our asses off, and then one of our guys in the truck in front of me fired an apple at the sergeant, yelling "Loser!" Unfortunately, he missed and hit the cop car. The net result was the original victim got off, and the idiot's truck became the new victim.

Story #87: Soldier of Fortune

In the early 1980's, Soldier of Fortune magazine was a pretty popular magazine with our guys - especially the characters who had a "Rambo-ized" view of their part-time profession. The magazine was full of all sorts of useful articles like "How To Modify Your AR-15 To Make It Fully Automatic" or "Jungle Camouflage Techniques". In the back were ads for military equipment, books on knife-throwing, etc. As well there was a "Mercenaries Wanted" section.

Sure enough, one of our guys (Burnette) who worked in the Quartermaster's section in our unit decided that it would be cool to go and fight as a mercenary in Rhodesia. Supposedly they needed gunners who could work British artillery, so this seemed like a great fit. Unfortunately, Burnette missed the fact that it was against Canadian law to fight as a mercenary. Consequently, his letter to the address in Rhodesia was promptly intercepted by the RCMP at the border and sent back to our commanding officer (CO). When he got called in to our CO's office and saw his letter sitting there, the blood drained from his face,

and he thought his life was over. However, he just got a lecture about being an idiot, and some sort of 3 month local punishment, versus going to the military prison in Edmonton.

Story #88: Chinooks

In the Ottawa area, there was the 450 Helicopter Squadron who flew Chinooks[†]. Never missing an opportunity to do things with our "brothers in arms" we used to routinely fly down to Fort Drum, NY for weekend exercises. Basically you had a choice of driving for 3 hours to get from Ottawa to Fort Drum, or flying with the boys from 450 and getting there in about 90 minutes. Unfortunately, it was not the most pleasant means of travel. We could fit two 105mm howitzers in a Chinook, and about 5 people down either side on cargo strap "seats". What made flying in these things SUCK was the following:

1) The turbine engines were extremely loud, requiring you to wear ear-defenders to deafen the dentist-drill whine.

2) There was a heavy smell of jet-engine exhaust throughout the cabin.

3) The blades made the light continuously flicker.

4) The only windows you could see out of were little round "cruise-ship" style portals that offered you a "beer-glass" view of your surroundings.

5) The pilots were maniacs who did their best to give the occupants a hell-ride full of heavy acceleration, intense turns, dives, etc.

[†] Those big two rotor military transport helicopters

I travelled with these clowns once. At the time I remember thinking "Wow! It will be so cool to ride in a Chinook." Wrongo!

After about 45 minutes, I was well acquainted with #1 - #4 above, but once we crossed the US border, #5 started. Being an aficionado of roller-coasters, I thought the pilot's stunts were pretty cool - except the "roller-coaster ride" didn't end. Plus one of my compadres across from me had curled up into a ball on the floor and was covered in puke. Trying to see what was happening through the window didn't help either, as you were either looking at sky, or seeing trees rushing towards you. Finally we made it to Fort Drum and escaped.

Unfortunately, with the 450 Squadron there was no one-way ticket, and if you went down with them, you had to come back with them, and this is where things got really interesting.

After the delightful 48 hours of no sleep, and covered in dust and sweat, we loaded the howitzers on the Chinooks and climbed in. Donning our ear-defenders, we waited in expectation as the gas-turbines reached speed, the cabin filled with exhaust fumes, the light started flickering and we started to ascend. About 20 feet off the ground, there was suddenly a loud "Bang!" and the back rotor failed! We found ourselves hanging almost vertically from the cargo-strap seats as we slammed back to the ground.

"Holy CRAP!" was all I thought, as the back gate hydraulics slowly opened, revealing the unimpressed face of the Flight Sergeant.

"Out!" he commanded, and we all scrambled out, happy to be alive.

"Wait in here" he said, gesturing to a small office, containing a few wooden chairs and not much else.

After four hours of staring at the floor, the Flight Sergeant reappeared in the doorway and barked "Everyone back on board!".

Since I am still alive, we obviously made it, but that was the end of me travelling with the 450.

Story #89: Borden

The summer after I joined, I signed up to get my Jeep licence. In the Canadian military, you had to have a separate license for every vehicle, and it didn't matter if you had a real driver's license or not: if you were on military business and were licensed to drive a certain vehicle, you could drive it, and supposedly the cops couldn't jack with you[†]. To me, this sounded really cool - sort of like the first step in obtaining a "License to Kill", so naturally I signed up. Plus I got paid.

The course was being held at Camp Borden, near Barry, Ontario (north of Toronto). Accommodations were naturally sleeping in a tent on a military air-mattress with mosquito netting. For some reason, I had failed to notice (probably due to never getting more than four hours of sleep on exercises) that the air mattresses the Canadian military issued (or at least the ones the reserves got) were total crap. Basically they had some sort of stopper that resembled what you would find on a rubber water-bottle, and after inflation they would proceed to slowly deflate over the next 5 hours. Nothing you could do would halt this

---

[†] Unfortunately, this wasn't exactly the segue into Grand Theft Auto that it sounded like, as if you screwed up and the cops pulled you over, they'd radio for the Military Police (aka "M-Pigs") and the party would be over real quick.

inevitable process, and the result was that when attempting to get something resembling a normal "non-exercise" sleep, you woke up around 4 am on the ground, and in Borden this also meant covered in ants.

The other thing I learned in Borden involved mosquito netting. For some reason - maybe the US Green Card system played a role - the mosquitoes in the US are basically lazy and have no real work ethic. In Canada however, the situation is much more dire - to the point that in my entire life, I was never able to sit on any back porch for more than 15 minutes after dusk without being eaten alive by mosquitoes[†]. Naturally, Borden offered all of the comforts of home in spades. Consequently, if you were going to enjoy your 5 hours of non-ant-covered sleep, you had to properly set up your mosquito-net. This was easier said than done, as any slight opening in the net would result in the inevitable, high-pitched "Zzzzz" sound in your ear within 15 minutes of trying to sleep.

It was maddening. At first you flailed around, attempting to kill the offending mosquito, but even if you achieved victory by mashing the bug against your now-reddened face, another one would take his fallen comrade's place within the next 15 minutes. Consequently, you were forced to get up with your flashlight (while your buddies in the tent who were more diligent than you with their nets cursed you out) and try and find the hole. Despite our Quartermaster's best attempts to drive us insane by issuing torn netting, you

---

[†] I particularly enjoyed May in eastern Canada, when you not only had the standard mosquito menace, but had the added pleasure of black flies. These little bastards would bite you and they had some sort of anti-coagulant in their saliva that made you continue to bleed after they bit you. I remember cutting my parent's lawn whilst fighting off mosquitoes and black flies, and at the end finishing with my arms slathered in blood. Good times.

eventually figured it out, and through a combination of duct tape, improvised sewing, and clever tucking of the netting under your constantly deflating air-mattress, you could eventually achieve "victory" over the evil mosquito horde - until you stretched your feet out and untucked the netting. Aaaah! In writing this I am still scarred.

After several weeks of this fun, I passed my TQ1[†] and received my first military driver's licence. Along the way, I got to help out shovelling potatoes into the mess-hall, and met some interesting characters who dug a 10 foot deep mine-shaft, complete with bracing into their tent floor - for no particularly good reason.

On the last night, we had an alcohol fueled party: a particularly good party. In fact, it was such a good party that we decided to roll some guy's wreck of a vehicle that he had driven up to Borden[‡]. What was particularly funny was that the guy actually hated his car and encouraged us to roll it. After trashing his car, we threw some toilet paper rolls in the trees and retired for 5 hours of uninterrupted sleep.

Next morning however, things were not so funny. The base commander was particularly unimpressed with the festivities from the night before, and called in the M-Pigs to investigate. It turned out that somebody had also slashed one of the tents, and this provided the impetus to unleash a full-on investigation into who did it.

First we had to stand on parade whilst we were all berated about being total bags of crap, and then after nobody confessed to any of the crimes, the M-Pigs showed up and

---

[†] Trade-Qualification 1

[‡] I guess you could also show up with your own mode of transportation, which never occurred to me

started their inquisition. Each of us (there must have been around 200 people) was led in front of a bunch of amateur Sherlock Holmeses and questioned about who did what. Nothing - nobody did anything.

OK - so back for round two. Still nothing. Apparently the slashed tent, rolled car, and toilet-papered trees were all the result of either an alien invasion, or some deranged homeless person. Finally - about 7 pm that night, the wannabe detectives admitted failure and we were allowed to leave.

Story #90: Deuce-and-a-Halfs

The ride to and from Borden to Ottawa was accomplished (by those of us not fortunate enough to have a rollable car) in the back of a deuce-and-a-half (the 2½ ton, 6-wheel drive, canvas-backed, troop-transport trucks I told you about earlier). These babies were the mainstay of our transport, and in addition to transporting troops on their delightful wooden benches, were also good for towing howitzers.

We - the lower ranking hoi-polloi - were relegated to the canvas-covered back, whilst two privileged members of our regiment got to sit up front in the cab on the bench seat along with the driver. Communication between the cab and our area was accomplished via a little sliding window, which conveniently locked from the cab-side.

Unfortunately, the deuce was rather limited in its speed. With the pedal to the metal, you could perhaps top out around 55 mph, and in this state the deuce was shaking and sounded like it was going to catch fire and explode. Consequently, what should have been a 5 hour journey back to Ottawa in a regular vehicle, took around 8 hours, putting our ETA into Ottawa around 3am.

As the night wore on, we inflated our air-mattresses and fell asleep on the floor. I was having the most pleasant dream, when all of a sudden I was awoken by a rude tossing. I looked through the little sliding window, and to my horror saw all three occupants of the cab with heads down, asleep.

"Wake up!" I screamed. Nothing.

I proceeded to bang on the window as we began drifting back onto the shoulder, and finally the sergeant in the middle woke up and realizing we were about to die, swung into action and grabbed the wheel, and screamed at the driver to wake up.

Upon awakening, the driver slammed the brakes on, promptly sending all of us cascading into the back wall of the deuce.

We were then all ordered out onto the shoulder of the highway, and made to do some jumping jacks to wake us up. Finally, after the sergeant was convinced the driver was fully awake, we proceeded on our journey.

Mercifully, when we got to Ottawa, the sergeant decided to just drop us at our houses. Being the last one, I got to sit in the cab and for fun did a rolling dive from the moving deuce onto my Dad's front lawn. It seemed cool at the time.

Story #91: Fort Drum Redux

The next time I visited lovely Fort Drum, I had my jeep license and was able to drive a jeep and enjoy the lovely 3 hours ride at 55 mph staring at the back of the deuce ahead of me in the convoy. Whilst noisy, it was still better than being stuck in the back of a deuce. The exercises were uneventful[†]- until departing on the Sunday journey home. I had driven perhaps 30 minutes to refuel when my

clutch died. Maybe it was the cable - who knew? The end result was that the jeep was essentially undriveable. It was here that a major decision had to be made - either stay in scenic Fort Drum until Monday or Tuesday when a mechanic could look at the jeep, or figure out how to start the thing in second, and bang-shift it into third[†]. Being 18, and my passenger expressing similar feelings about the charms of Fort Drum, the answer was obvious: drive it home. We also had the genius idea that we would avoid stopping again by refueling whilst driving. Since we had no canvas top, we figured that my buddy could crawl back and whilst leaning over the side, fill up the tank without us having to pull over. To that end we loaded up a couple of more 5 gallon jerry-cans of fuel in the back (essentially making us a mobile bomb), and worked on push-starting the jeep.

The idea was to start it in neutral, and then get it rolling fast enough to jam it into second without the clutch. After two or three failed attempts, and both of us covered in sweat, I finally jammed it into second, and I was off - leaving my partner running behind! Crap!

I circled back and after a couple of passes by him at idle, he managed to dive in, and we were off. We headed out onto the highway on-ramp in second and as I approached the highway, tried to bang-shift it into third. Double crap! The shifter was stuck in neutral, and we began to lose speed! I drifted onto the shoulder and fought with the shifter - no luck!!

"Whoosh!" A transport truck blew past us, blowing his horn at our erratic driving.

[†] And by uneventful, I mean the standard two days of no sleep, freezing at night, and being eaten by mosquitoes

[†] It was the classic Willy's 3-speed

Fortunately I managed to get it back into second, picked up speed in the gravel and tried again. Finally after a couple of attempts, I found the right shift point, and we lurched into third!! We were saved until the border.

At the border, we had to bring it to a halt by killing the engine, and pushed it through the line in customs, getting to repeat the whole starting and shifting to third again. This time though I knew the shift points, and it was much less painful.

About 2/3 of the way into it, we had to add some fuel, and slowing down as much as I could, my buddy managed to get about half the can poured into the tank - which was enough to get us home. By the time we hit Ottawa, we were more or less ignoring red lights, and doing anything to avoid going into second. But we made it!

Story #92: The Deuce

The next step in my driving license quest was a license for the deuce. This thing (as I mentioned earlier) was a six-wheel drive, Korean-war work-horse that had an automatic transmission. Low-range was six-wheel drive, and high-range was only driving the back 4 wheels. To get my license, I had to be able to demonstrate complete driving skills in reverse, using only mirrors, and the driving test involved parallel-parking the pig. It was tough, but I passed. Finally, I could enjoy the comforts of a heated cab (versus the breezy jeep).

I have to admit it was pretty fun. A deuce could drive through a forest and take out pretty much any tree smaller than 4" diameter, but in the process you typically ripped off the exhaust, which went up the side of the passenger door. Not my problem!

Figure 5.8 **Deuce towing a howitzer (**Tyler Brenot**)**

Typically when travelling in a convoy on exercises, you rolled back the tarp behind the cab, and two soldiers would stand on either side looking for enemy airplanes. If one was "spotted", the command "Disperse" was yelled[†] and you got to head into whatever undergrowth that existed, plowing down trees, and 90% of the time ripping off the exhaust. It was awesome.

Story #93: Connaught Lawn

The final step in my military license quest was to get a license to tow a howitzer behind a deuce (a TQ2). As soon as I racked up enough hours on the TQ1 deuce license, I signed up for the TQ2.

Unfortunately, most of this course involved spending weekends backing a deuce with a howitzer down dirt roads. The result was severe neck pain looking through the little window in the back. The favorite place to do this training was the Connaught Rifle range to the west of Ottawa.

[†] Or something to this effect. Basically every odd vehicle would head of the road right, and the even would head left.

When I took my course, it was early spring and the ground was saturated with snow melt. Towards the end of the course, I had gotten pretty good at backing up, and the sergeant with me decided we could stop backing up and head home. To facilitate a rapid departure, I did a U-turn on the base commander's front lawn.

Big mistake! The deuce promptly sank into the mud!

"No problem I thought - just stick it into 6-wheel drive mode".

Wrongo! My deuce promptly sunk up to it's axles in the mud, and I was screwed. I went out, boots sinking into the mud beneath the grass. Disconnecting the howitzer from the deuce, I was able to churn my way off the lawn, and then with my winch pull the howitzer out. Unfortunately at this point, the front lawn had two muddy trenches running the length of it.

"Whatever" I thought. The gardener would fix it.

Wrong again! The base commander got a call Monday morning, and my Monday evening was spent with a shovel repairing the ruined lawn.

Story #94: The Empire Strikes Back

The summer after Borden, I took a posting to Camp Shilo, near Brandon, Manitoba for the summer as the quartermaster's driver. It was a lazy staff job, and consisted of sitting around a lot, and driving stuff in a deuce once in a while.

There were several interesting things about Shilo. One was that they rented it out to the German army (I guess the scenery reminded them of the Russian steppe), and they had new Leopard II tanks with servo-tracking and laser

sights. The result is that these douches proceeded to shoot the hell out of all of the range markers - just because they could. Since I was in a staff position, I got to hear the complaints from the maintenance guys who had to replace all of these shot up markers.

Also in the mix, were the barracks. My buddy and I were by ourselves in a room that had four bunk-beds, and then after about 2 weeks, two old reprobates showed up. These were career army guys who had been up and down the career ladder, and were currently both busted back to corporal for some stupidity they had done. Neither of them seemed to care, and were pretty "easy come, easy go" travellers on the road of life. They promptly taught us how to play cribbage for money - which allowed them to immediately start relieving us of our cash. Even worse, they decided to challenge my buddy and me to a game of horse-shoes (metal spikes stuck in the ground 40 feet apart at which you had to throw horse-shoes, and the shoe closest to the spike won the round). We thought we'd kick their ass and bet accordingly. Yes - you guessed it - they kicked our asses and proceeded to take us for about $40 each. It was my first experience with the adage "Old age and treachery will always beat youth and exuberance".

One day, we were offered the chance to drive in a convoy that had to take a whole bunch of stuff back to the Winnipeg Armory. "The Empire Strikes Back" had just been released after a 5 year hiatus from the original Star Wars, and my buddy and I were crazy to see this. We begged our boss (a Warrant officer) to let us see this, and she said that as long as we unloaded and were back before morning, she didn't care. YES!! We were stoked.

The ride from Brandon to Winnipeg was roughly 3 hours long on a straight divided concrete highway, through flat farmland. Going there towing a howitzer, we found that

with the pedal to the metal, and doing about 58 mph, the spacing in the concrete slabs set up this nice resonance between the deuce and the howitzer, causing them both to bounce. It was 3 hours of kidney-pounding fun, and when we got there we were barely able to walk.

We worked like mad-men, and after unloading the deuce it was 10:30pm at night. We talked with the local armory guy, and were supposed to take some military Ford Econoline panel wagon back, so we queued it up, and heading off in the deuce, found a drive-in that was doing a midnight showing of "The Empire Strikes Back". For some reason, they made us park in the back.

A 2:30am, we left the drive-in[†], swapped the deuce for the Econoline van, and headed for Shilo.

Now if you are doing the math, you will realize that we are getting in around 5:30am, and that I have to drive 3 hours in the middle of the night down perfectly straight, flat 4-lane highway. It was the hardest drive of my life. We both stopped and bought some coffee, and then my partner immediately fell asleep, despite his heartfelt promises to stay awake and keep me from falling asleep.

About an hour into it, I started to hallucinate, and saw giant 1000' high birch forests closing in on the road from all sides. I opened the windows, slapped myself, all to no avail. Somehow, I managed to make it without falling asleep, and we returned to Shilo for 30 minutes of sleep.

[†] After watching the movie, I decided that I wanted to build the Death-Star and decided to go into electrical engineering, versus mechanical engineering.

Story #95: Winter Camping

One winter weekend we went to Fort Drum (typically we went on exercises somewhere once a month to burn off several hundred artillery shells at $600 a crack[†] - Canadian taxpayer money well spent). This time it was not just crappy canvas jackets stained with some Korean war dude's blood - it was real-deal arctic warfare, full-on white winter equipment: actual winter parkas, snow pants, white helmet covers, boots, gloves, etc. The whole nine-yards - and this stuff was actually warm. We also got thermal sleeping bags, air-mattresses that worked, and a metal foil sheet to put under them. I was stoked.

When we got there, we looked like Imperial Storm troopers, which I thought added a particularly cool vibe to the exercise.

After setting up, and a few winter artillery barrages, us Storm Troopers were allowed to make a camp fire out of the used wooden artillery crates. At the same time, as part of an arctic warfare exercise, we were issued rat-packs (ration packs). As expected, and being the proverbial hind-tit of the Canadian military, they pawned off their expiring rat-packs on us. It was like going into a time warp and tasting the preserved meal-plan of 1964. There were toothpaste tubes of ketchup, mayonnaise, and mustard. Surprisingly, there was a 28oz can of some sort of cake, which was actually not that bad. Consequently, most of the contents were discarded, but the "can-o'-cake" was devoured by all.

Now - you the reader must know that I'm not telling some story about burning artillery crates in the winter, and rat-packs without some darker purpose. Well, after the

---

[†] 1970's dollars

"can-o'-cakes" were all devoured, and the other dubious food-stuffs discarded, some fool decided to throw a tube of mayonnaise into the fire. Nobody noticed, until about 3 minutes later it exploded, blasting its boiling mayonnaise contents at some poor victim. Awesome! Russian roulette with old condiments!

Over the next hour, we proceeded to get blasted (and a bit burned) with all the old condiments until a sergeant showed up and told us to end the revelry.

Story #97: Gagetown

My final summer in the Reserves was spent in Gagetown, New Brunswick (Canada's Arkansas) posted with the Airborne Artillery. These douche-bags were basically Hell's Angels in uniform. They were big, nasty animals who liked to fight, and had little appreciation for university-going Reserve scum like me. I remember pulling in and seeing Rambo-like dudes carving bed frames out of trees they had cut down with their Bowie-knives. It was a less-than-pleasant experience that ended my desire to ever have anything to do with the military again. However, there are some pretty humourous stories from this experience.

The first was the ride there, which took two days at 50-55 mph. By the time we had got there, we had lost almost 10% of our vehicles to mechanical failure. It became obvious to me that the way to destroy the Canadian military was to threaten to attack them at some spread-out locations along the border, and after about 3 or 4 long journeys in a convoy there would be nothing left.

Another humourous reminiscence was my attempting to light an immersion heater. We all had to do sentry duty throughout various nights, and the person assigned to the

2am - 6am shift had to light something called an immersion heater to make hot-water for shaving, etc. Now an immersion heater is essentially a U-shaped tube that has a grate at the bottom on the intake side of the tube, and a canister of gasoline that drips down onto the grate. Once it is running, you get a fire burning on the grate from the gas and it heats the water. The tricky part is getting it going.

Now I was shown how it worked: you dripped some gas on an asbestos wad (nice huh?) that was on the end of a long coat-hanger wire, then lit it, turned on the drip and stuck the burning wad down the intake tube. Simple - right?

Wrong! Inevitably you got too much gas down there, and then when you finally stuck the burning wad down - "WHAM!" - a blast of flame would shoot up, and you suddenly had no facial hair whatsoever.

As you can guess, I immediately experienced this depilatory pleasure, and showing up in the mess tent at 7:30am, found everybody laughing at me. Apparently I had a bright red face and no eye-brows or eye-lashes!

Appendix B: Cars

I am writing this appendix on behalf of my son Augustus, who is now learning how to drive, and loves cars. Hopefully you'll find it as enjoyable as he does.

Story #98: My First Car Accident

My first car accident occurred whilst going out to pick up some pizza on a snowy night. Being sixteen, this was awesome, as I could practice my hand-brake turns in my parent's diesel Volkswagon Rabbit. This 48 HP pig-of-a-car was the most underpowered vehicle ever sold in the North American market, but hey - it got great mileage! It also was front-wheel drive and slid really nicely around corners with the hand-brake, which locked up the rear wheels.

Leaving early for the pizza, I immediately headed into a neighbourhood with lots of turns and no salt on the road, making for perfect "Steve McQueen" conditions. Ten minutes later, I put the Rabbit into a curb, and bent the A-arm so the wheel was munched into the fender. Having no cell-phone, I started ringing door-bells until somebody let me phone my parents from their house. It cost $385 of my hard-earned money to fix. (I shovelled driveways for money in the winter).

Story #99: The Capri

I have already told you a little about this gem in Section 5.1, but I will now elucidate. At age 17, I had about $2000 to my name, and wanted a car - badly. My Dad knew nothing about cars, but one of the guys who worked in his group said he had a really cool vehicle he'd let go for $1500 - a 1974 2.8L Ford Capri (sold in the US I believe as

The "Letter Guy" and Other Stories

a Mercury Capri?). I saw it, I was in love, and love was blind. The guy was a total idiot and honestly thought it was in good condition, except for some rust.

If he maintained it, the mechanic just took his money and did nothing. The oil appeared to have never been changed, and the rings were worn. On top of this, there were large amounts of rust that needed body work (you can tell from Figure 5.1).

Anyway, I didn't care, and set about with advice from my friend Sandy to tear the thing apart, with the intention of turning it into a hot-rod. My goal was to strip all of the smog abatement equipment from the car (which in 1974 basically meant a charcoal canister and an air injection system to dilute the exhaust), overbore the engine, install a high-rise cam, aluminum pistons, headers, a split Weber carburetor, and then see how much extra horse-power I could generate. In parallel, I would repair the rust issues with the body.

I figured that I could have all this done in the summer, before university started in the fall. Wow - was I wrong . . .

As I tore the thing apart in my Dad's driveway, I started to meet an entirely different bunch of neighbours. Neighbours that my family had never seen before, but were very interested in the car, and full of all sorts of advice: most of it worthless.

I basically had no idea what I was doing, but what I did know was that it was going to be a lot of work. To help ease the load, I traded my brother 20% of the Capri, which was supposed to allow him to drive the vehicle once a week, in exchange for slave labor[†]. I soon regretted this, as Dave's enthusiasm for driving the vehicle rapidly waned, as did his productivity. One of his tasks was to carefully label every

piece from the car with masking tape and store the parts in our shed, but even this was too much for him. Finally I "gave" him back his 20% and let him stop pretending to work. I was on my own. My friend Sandy was also less than enthusiastic about helping: While dispensing advice was easy, grinding off rust with an angle grinder was a lot less fun.

My Dad was horrified when he finally understood that the engine-less wreck on axle jacks in his driveway was going to be there through the winter. He also noticed that his electricity bill had almost doubled due to constant power-tool use.

I beavered away and slowly finished the body work, eventually becoming an expert on Bondo. I used to go down to the local speed-shop and drool over Capri parts I could buy - if only I had the money. However, I had joined the Canadian Artillery reserves earlier that year and did have some cash-flow - albeit slow. One by one, I accumulated the magic pieces that would turn the wreck into a super-car. Unfortunately, one of the first things I bought was a pair of calfskin driving gloves, which quickly became a cruel joke every time I looked out at the hulk in the driveway. The gloves mocked me.

Throughout the winter of 1979-1980, I slowly acquired the money to get the engine over-bored and the performance parts installed. When I finally had enough money, I rented an engine hoist, loaded the engine onto a piece of plywood in the back of the diesel Rabbit (which was not very happy at having its suspension bottomed out) and took it to a garage that did this kind of work (I'm trying to remember

---

† Ha! In retrospect, it seems that little changed from the days of trading gravel for his treasures!

the name - I think it was Jim Stagra Automotive), and handed everything over. Three weeks later it was ready.

I re-rented the engine hoist, and after re-torturing the Rabbit's suspension, spent the weekend installing the engine, reaping the benefits of Dave's unenthusiastic part-labeling from the previous year. What Dave hadn't half-assed labeled on greasy masking tape with a blue pen, with descriptive names like "Thing from front of engine", winter had taken care of. It was like trying to do a jigsaw puzzle upside down. Eventually, I got everything reassembled that needed to go on (i.e. radiator, alternator, water-pump), but still had a bunch of bolts left over that gave me a vague uneasy feeling of impending calamity.

Around 9 pm one Sunday night, the beast (sans mufflers, which I viewed as unimportant) was ready to start. Timing light and screw-driver in hand, we (several of the "parallel universe" neighbors had also shown up for the event) cranked the engine. After a few coughs and sputters, it caught. We adjusted the timing, set the carburetor and Man! - did it sound good. And by good, I meant loud! It idled with the standard muscle-car "Thrump-tha-thrump" and was everything I dreamed of. Finally - after a year, I had my dream car. Well - almost. There were a few little matters involving brakes, doors, wheels, and paint. And - oh yeah - mufflers.

My Dad appeared about a minute after the deafening roar of the engine filled our peaceful neighbourhood, and demanded that we turn the car off, as it was after 9pm. Frankly it was a good thing he did stop me, as the neoprene gas line I had run was draped over the header, and during the engine revving it had melted and was now spewing gas onto the hot headers. Phew! Dodged a bullet! Didn't need a repeat of the snowmobile!

Later that night, Dad decided to mention that the vehicle needed mufflers - like now. I told him I had some - cheap straight-pipe Thrush mufflers, that resembled big silencers. After installing them, not much changed - plus the exhaust didn't quite exit the under-carriage of the vehicle without some additional piping, which I could not afford. Happily my Dad's aversion to attention-focussing noise caused him to cough up the $450 to get a set of custom mufflers made.

Several weeks later, I was finally on the road. The thing was awesome - I took it to a dyno where it clocked in at around 270 HP, and it did 0-60 mph in around 6 seconds! (I figured this out on my university's private roads on the weekend).

So - all good? Just get it painted, and "Bob's your Uncle?". I wish.

Figure 5.9 **The finished Capri - not bad, eh?**

Story #100: Cops

Nothing is more of a cop magnet than a teenager driving a primer and Bondo-covered hot-rod. I got pulled over roughly every 3 weeks, and inevitably, they'd find something.

"Where are your bumpers?" or "Your left running light is out."

It was maddening. I was suddenly a second-class citizen, unfairly marked and persecuted because of my vehicle!

Story #101: Burning Oil

After about 3 months of driving, I started burning oil. At first I did what every normal male does - ignore it, and pretend that there was nothing wrong. Unfortunately, ignoring it became impossible, and it soon turned into "Fill up the oil, and check the gas". This combined with a total loss of horsepower and compression, led me to the sorry conclusion that something was wrong with the aluminum pistons. I yanked the heads and made the sickening discovery that the wrist pins in the pistons were floating free, and had cut grooves in the cylinder walls. I was screwed, and the only solution was to install much-hated cylinder sleeves.

I towed the Capri[†] down to the garage that did the work, and tried to get them to fix it as it was "their problem".

"No kid - you gave us the parts. We put them in. Your problem."

[†] Using the perfectly illegal technique of a rope behind the Rabbit. Too short and you'd crash into the Rabbit. Too long, and you'd scythe down pedestrians on the corner. A tricky bit of business, but cheaper than a tow-bar!

I left the Capri in their lot, and periodically showed up, hoping it would be magically fixed. No such luck. Finally my Dad showed up, and after 15 minutes of negotiating, he and the owner agreed on a price, and my Dad offered me a loan to cover the cost - with my soul as collateral. Suddenly Dad could start dictating how I lived my life. If I didn't like it - then pay the money back. What a nightmare. Four week later, I got the car back, and 6 months later I repaid my Dad.

Story #102: Other Issues

Well - it turns out that automotive engineers actually do something. In my doubling of the horse-power, there were a few things I failed to address:

1) Valve-float: it turns out that when you install a highly eccentric cam-shaft (i.e. as opposed to nice, fat, egg-shaped lobes on the cam-shaft that slowly open and close the valves, you have a long, thin eccentric-shape that slams the valves open and closed as fast as possible). Unfortunately, the factory valve-springs are not designed for this, and when doing time trials on my university roads[†], I'd notice that at around 6000 rpm, the horse-power would end - all because the springs weren't strong enough to close the valves fast enough!! Ugh!

2) Fuel pump too small: another nasty thing that would happen around 6000 rpm (right after the horse-power ended), the engine would stall. Turns out I didn't have enough pump capacity in my stock mechanical fuel-pump, and the float-bowl in the carburetor would go dry. Double Ugh!!

[†] I figured that since the university was private property, the real cops couldn't touch me there, and the rental cops could never catch me.

3) Frame separation: it also turns out that the Capri had a quasi-unit body chassis - which meant that it had some frame, and the rest of the structure was the actual car body, with crimping for strength (the advent of computer analysis caused this!!). Well, doubling the horse-power was not something the engineers had in mind when they designed this thing, and after about 1 year, the frame pieces started to tear away from the body. Triple Ugh!!!

The net result was that while my hopped up Capri looked good, and could get pretty fast to 60 mph, there were also some bad things that happened around 65 mph, and the body was slowly tearing itself apart.

Story #103: The Shifter

Given the above, I used to take all of my tools with me whenever I went anywhere with the Capri, as it seemed to have a mean-time-between failure (MTBF in engineering-speak) of around 4 hours. Something was always breaking, or needing adjustment.

One time, I decided to take it to Kingston for the weekend - about 90 minutes south of Ottawa on the St. Lawrence. Tools in the trunk, driving gloves on - I headed south on Hwy 16 - a two lane highway, full of slow drivers, just waiting to be passed[†]. About 10 minutes in, I pulled out to pass a line of idiots, slammed the shifter from 4th into 3rd (it was a 4-speed) and the shifter broke off in my hand, with the transmission in neutral, and me in the opposing lane. "Crap!" I thought, and having lost speed, I drifted over onto the opposing shoulder and stopped. Looking down into the shifter slot[‡], I saw there was a 1/2" stub of metal that used

---

[†] In fact the same highway from my brush with death in the deuce in Story #90.

to attach to the shifter I was holding in my hand. Fortunately, I had in my tools an 11mm deep socket, which I was able to use with an extender to get all four gears. Unfortunately, the socket was too wide to get reverse - which was away and up from 3rd and 4th. Consequently, I drove for over a year without reverse before I could locate a used shifter. Apparently I wasn't the only one with this problem. Probably the same douche-bags that designed the unit-body!

Anyway, during that year I got pretty adept at parking so that reverse was not required. An added benefit was that I could take the ersatz shifter with me into a store and leave the car running. Good luck trying to steal that thing!

Story #104: The Loose Seat

For quite a while, I drove the Capri without putting the bolts back into the passenger seat. It looked quite normal, but upon accelerating, the occupant would find themselves rolling around in the back seat. I think I just enjoyed the practical-joke aspect of it. Needless to say, I was going to university one day in 3rd year, and I saw my electronics professor at the bus-stop, and offered him a ride . . . Amazingly I still passed, but I also attribute it to the fact he was British and was used to dealing with dubious vehicles.

Story #105: The House of Guitars

I have to tell this story, just because of its sheer craziness. Growing up in Ottawa, after we finally wore down my Dad enough to get a decent TV and cable in 1976[†], we were

---

[‡] It was open, versus having a rubber boot

[†] Prior to this we had this piece of tweed furniture from Fleetwood that also doubled as a black-and-white television. If the tubes were good, the tuner properly adjusted, and the antenna positioned just right, you could get two TV stations: CBC and CTV.

able to get TV stations from Rochester and Plattsburg in New York. The Rochester station was particularly interesting, as they routinely ran ads for this out-of-control record store called "The House of Guitars". There were ads with some guy in a leather jacket wearing sun-glasses and easter-bunny ears jumping around in front of some WWII scene with AC/DC's Hell's Bells playing, and him saying "Hop, Hop, Hop". I had to see this place. Nobody I knew had ever gone there, so I set out on a pilgrimage in the Capri. My coworkers gave me money to buy House of Guitars T-shirts which at the time had a target on them with the words "Kill Me - I Ain't Ever Died Before". Totally cool!

Well things went well until I was approaching this intersection on the two-lane highway under Lake Ontario that led to Rochester. It had a stop-light and a gas station on the corner to my right. Just before this was a house, with a car backing down the driveway. Unfortunately, this car did not stop, but backed straight onto the highway, where I was approaching at 65 mph! CRAP!!!

I leaned on my horn, and swerved into the ditch to dodge T-boning the idiot in the car, and promptly lost control of the Capri. I got it out of the ditch, but then wound up sliding sideways through the gas-pumps of the service station, coming to a stop on the far side of the pumps. Phew! Still alive - and even better, no scrapes on the Capri.

After I went back to yell at the idiot, it turned out to be a 90 year-old lady who was completely frazzled, and yelling at her was useless. In fact she almost backed her car into the Capri again!

As a sequel to this story, when I finally got to Rochester, it was the most bizarre experience. I knew the city from the TV station, and recognized half of the landmarks I passed (i.e. the War Memorial, the Irondoquiot Mall, etc.) but I had

no idea how they fit together. I only knew they were in Rochester.

I visited the House Of Guitars and it really was that cool. Pretty much anybody in rock has been there and signed their name on a wall, and the T-shirts were great. I also found out that the Pabst brewery was downstream from the Kodak plant - good news if you wondered why Pabst Blue Ribbon turns dark in the sunlight! Just kidding . . .

Story #106: The Demise of the Capri

One sad morning, I got up to find that thieves had broken into the Capri and basically destroyed the interior trying to remove the stereo and speakers. Outraged, I went to my insurance, and found that the write-off value of the vehicle was $700. Apparently, you needed to have some sort of special insurance to dodge the salvage price cap. Quadruple Ugh!!!! I took the $700 and never spent more than $100 on a vehicle after that for the next 5 years.

Story #107: The Toyota Corona

One other fact which I neglected to mention about the Capri was that it was essentially undriveable in snow. The light weight, and high horse-power made it a disaster. Consequently, I was forced to come up with an alternative form of transportation during the winter. My salvation came in the form of a beat-up family car that my friend's Dad was selling - a Toyota Corona[†]. They wanted $100 for this baby, and since it ran, and was standard - I took it. In fact it didn't even need a key, as the ignition lock was broken and any slot-head screwdriver could start the thing. Unfortunately this led to idiot friends of mine endlessly pranking me by moving the vehicle.

[†] Yes - it's Corona, and not Corolla, despite them being similar. Not sure if it was sold in the US?

Figure 5.10 **The Toyota Corona**

Now the first order of business in buying any used car is to get it to pass a safety inspection, which on old vehicles primarily meant:

1) No holes in the body from the exterior into the interior

2) Brakes, tires, lights, shocks, etc.

The second one was pretty straightforward, and in the worst case involved having to buy some new or used replacement parts. However the first one was more onerous, as it involved some actual body-work, or at least should have. The reason I say "should have" is that you could create something that looked pretty close to body-work with some cardboard and a wonderful product that was sold in Canada called Bulldog Grip Roofing Cement. This stuff was essentially undercoat, and if you glued a piece of cardboard over the hole with this stuff, and then slathered it on top and bottom, it would harden in a couple of days and hold up to a minor pokes with a screwdriver - which would get you past the inspection. It frankly even lasted not bad, as long as you made sure to

leave no holes! The expression my friends and I had when looking at a hole in a car body was "Just Bulldog it".

Now when I took possession of the Corona, there were a lot of places that got Bulldogged, but unfortunately, one of the problem areas were the floorboards, both of which were pretty much rusted out. Since this required actual metal, I bought a sheet of aluminum and cut out two floorboard pieces, beat them into shape, and then pop-riveted them into place. Then I proceeded to Bulldog the bottom - and I was ready to go.

Over the next several years, I squeezed every bit of life out of that vehicle. It ran, but it was tired, and wanted badly to go to the wrecking yard. But I had no plans to give it the release it wanted.

Story #108: The Corona Floorboards

The first thing to go on the Corona were the floor-boards. What? Didn't I just fix them?? Yes, but . . .

In any city where they have regular snow-fall and the average temperature is above the melting point of salt-water (around -17°C), they'll liberally dose the roads with salt to keep them clear of ice. Unfortunately not until the late 1980's did vehicle undercoating technology develop to a point where it could withstand salt spray throughout the winter. The Corona was no exception, and outside of where I Bulldogged it, it was vigorously corroding away. Unfortunately, saltwater also acts as a great electrolyte, and add some aluminum and steel to the saltwater, and the steel goes into turbo-rust mode. In a little over 5 months of winter, my floorboard repair was done. I unfortunately found this out the hard way when I hit a pot-hole and my driver's side floorboard promptly fell out treating me to an intense slush-spray from the front tire.

Ugh! It turns out I only Bulldogged the bottom, and forgot about boots covered in slush melting into the carpets. Worse, I was going out to a nice restaurant and was wearing a suit . . .

Story #109: The Corona Exhaust System

The next thing to die on the Corona was the exhaust system. At the time I lived in this total dive of an apartment building, two blocks past the Rochester Street off-ramp heading east on the Queensway (Hwy 17 and the main highway through Ottawa), and one block to the right. One day, coming home from work, as I exited the Queensway at Rochester Street, I heard a very loud scraping noise. Crap - probably the exhaust. Slowing to a stop at the lights at the bottom of the Rochester off-ramp, I suddenly felt the entire rear of my car "pole-vault". Sure enough, I went out and there was my rusty muffler sticking out from under the rear bumper. I quickly solved this problem by breaking the muffler off by jumping on it, and then kicking it into the gutter. Whilst doing this, I noticed the driver in the car behind me was laughing his ass off.

At this point, the Corona needed some sort of exhaust system that would get the exhaust out from underneath all the Bulldogged holes. Now the key to extracting the most amount of savings from of a vehicle that you know is destined for the wrecking yard, is to never spend an unnecessary cent on it. Consequently, the replacement exhaust system I installed consisted of some flexible, grey steel tubing suspended with some coat-hangers. The net result was something that looked (and acted) like an elephant's trunk protruding from the back of the car.

Story #110: The Corona Fenders

The next thing to go on the Corona were the fenders. The attach points connecting the bottom of the fender to the

frame had rusted out on both sides, and the humourous result was that they would both start to flap like wings when I drove down the highway. Finally this behaviour got so intense that I decided I had better fix it, or risk completely losing the fenders.

Back at my auto-shop (aka the apartment parking lot), I slid the crank jack that came with the car under the frame by the passenger's door and started cranking: Crank, up. Crank, up. Crank, nothing. Crank, (crunch noise). Crank down! Aaah! The frame under the passenger side was rusted through where I was cranking. Furthermore, upon inspection I found that there was nothing unrusted to attach the fenders to.

OK - on to plan B - binder twine. I solved the problem by tying the fenders to the engine mounts, and no more flying car.

Story #111: The Death of the Corona

While there are some easy dodges for most minor mechanical issues, once the electrical system of a car starts to go, the end is near. I'm not talking about a car with an intact wiring harness that needs a new alternator - I'm talking about a vehicle whose wires are basically cracked, faded insulation covering green dust. Touch these wires, and you immediately get more issues than the one you set out to fix.

Well, coming home from work on the Queensway one dark winter day, about 3 miles from my exit the engine started to splutter. Crap! I shut off the headlights, and the engine picked back up[†]. I was good for a few more miles, and was able to keep the engine running until my exit, at which point it died. Fortunately, it was downhill to my apartment, and I was able to coast through the red light at the bottom of the

ramp, down another block, and around the corner into my parking lot. I knew the end of the Corona was nigh.

Having expected this issue, I had already located a wrecking yard that would pay $25 to come and get any vehicle, and $35 if the vehicle would run. The night before I siphoned most of the gas from the tank, and charged the battery. To dodge the Corona's decayed wreck of an electrical system, I wired the output of the alternator directly to the input of the distributor - effectively bypassing everything, and then cranked up the idle so that I could run the engine without my brand-new battery[†].

Fifteen minutes prior to the wrecker showing up, I started the engine and removed the battery. OK - ready for my $35! The look of disappointment on the wrecker driver's face as he handed over the money was palpable, and so very sweet. My Toyota Corona had served me well, and as I wiped away an invisible tear, I was almost touched as it headed off into the sunset.

Story #112: The Volkswagon Rabbit

After the death of the Corona, I needed a new car, and Lo and Behold, Providence provided in the form of my parent's old Volkswagon Diesel Rabbit (Story #98). They had finally had enough of this pig's underpowered fun, and had decided to buy a Toyota Camry to replace it. Consequently they were more than happy to unload it on me for $100 (it can be seen lounging in my Dad's driveway

---

[†] This wasn't just a lucky guess, as curious things had been happening with the battery charging indicator, which also led to my education in the field of corroding wires, and my splurging on a new battery.

[†] My Uncle Garry, upon reading this, commented that my techniques were very similar to my relatives Bert and Bernard (Appendix C). I guess you can run from DNA, but you can't hide . . .

in the back of Figure 5.1). Thus began a relatively short, but interesting journey.

I already knew the thing was underpowered, and you basically drove it with your foot to the floor, regardless of what gear it was in. Second, what used to be a bargain for diesel fuel when my parents bought the thing in 1978, was now actually more expensive than regular gasoline. Third, I discovered that if the weather went down below -25°C, even if you plugged in the car to keep the engine block warm, you only had a ~50% chance of starting it before the battery died heating the glow-plugs. Basically I hated this thing.

And it appeared that the Rabbit hated me as well. Within a year, I punched a hole in one of the cylinders[†], making it basically undriveable without carrying large quantities of oil around. I found this out on Hwy 401 going 140 km/h up a hill in 4th gear, when a sudden loss of power and clouds of black smoke out the exhaust provided a clue as to what was wrong. After limping home, I had had enough of diesel engines, and decided to convert the pig to a gasoline Rabbit.

I set about trying to find an engine, and as luck would have it, one of my Dad's colleagues at work had an old VW Rabbit that he said wouldn't run, but was willing to sell for $50. I headed out to look at it, found that it seemed to be in reasonable shape, and handed over $50 for the title.

Enlisting a friend's help to tow this back to my house[‡], I hooked up the standard illegal tow-rope and headed home. Once I got it home, I started assessing how I would

---

[†] Probably from driving it with the pedal always to the floor

[‡] I now had a small house in a suburb west of Ottawa called Kanata

affect the part transfer process from the new "dead" Rabbit to my old diesel. Following some basic inspection, it occurred to me that this "dead" Rabbit was potentially in better shape than my diesel version. Consequently after some basic debug, I figured out that the only thing wrong with the "dead" Rabbit was it needed a new alternator and battery. Ten minutes later, with the alternator and battery from the diesel Rabbit, and some Quick Start, I had the gas Rabbit running. Awesome - I had just bought a running gas Rabbit in good shape for $50! I quickly transferred all of the other required parts from the diesel Rabbit to the gas Rabbit.

Now I could have just sold the Diesel Rabbit to the wreckers, but since I wanted the tires which were in good shape, I figured why not cut the car into pieces with a cutting torch? Makes perfect sense - doesn't it?

I thought so - and having recently gotten may hands on some oxy-acetylene torches and tanks, this was the perfect excuse for some serious cutting action!

Unfortunately, things were not as pleasant as I hoped. It turns out that undercoating burns really well, and with all of the charm of a tire fire. I found you could heat it up and then scrape the gooey mass off with a plaster-knife before cutting, but it made a mess and you still tended to get something caught on fire. My recommendation? Don't do it. There's far too much smoke and fire, and it isn't like you can just blast through a section of car with the torches blazing. And don't get me started on upholstery . . .[†]

After a couple of weeks, I had burned pieces of Rabbit scattered around my yard in the snow. The next door neighbor was cool, but you could tell his patience for my transforming his piece of suburban paradise into Wilkes-Barre, PA was not high. Consequently, I borrowed

a pick-up truck from my Dad and took it all to the dump. After paying fees to unload the burned wreckage and the cost of the oxygen and acetylene - it was unclear if I actually even saved money on the tires.

Story #113: The Date

After about 6 months, I began dating this girl at work, and picked her up in my gas Rabbit. She met me at the curb of her father's house, and when she opened the passenger door, I realized that nobody had ever opened this door since I took possession of the car. The door slowly creaked open, with no oil on its hinges - like a sound effect from a coffin opening in a horror movie. Once open, you could see the collection of cobwebs across the passenger seat. Nice! Regardless my new girlfriend laughed and things went OK, but she never forgot that first date.

Story #114: The Cortina and the Ice Sheet

About 2 years later, things were beginning to break on the Rabbit. The clutch went, then issues started with the throttle-body and fuel-injection system. Plus I had married the girl from Story #113 and had much less interest

---

† There is an interesting anecdote I heard later from a friend after relating my "burning undercoat" story. He was into hot-rods, and was welding something on his car in his Dad's garage when the undercoating caught on fire. Fortunately, he was able to put it out, but unfortunately not before the smoke pouring from his Dad's garage signaled a helpful neighbour to call 911. Even though he had pushed the smoking car out into his driveway, the firemen upon arriving proceeded to rip the drywall from the walls and ceiling of the garage with their axes (yes - that's what that claw on their axes is for), and then puncture all of his Dad's paint cans - just to ensure the fire was out. Apparently it was a liability thing, and they were not able to leave without ensuring the fire was out, and my friend was totally screwed. It was a long wait until his father got home from work.

spending my free time repairing junk. Around this time one of her aunts was selling an old brown Ford Cortina for $500, so I sold the Rabbit for $100 and we bought this.

In order not to bore you, the Reader, I'll get to the point. This thing ran fine, but one snowy morning I was travelling to work down the Queensway. The snow from the night before had given way to intense freezing rain, and finally rain. This yielded a thick layer of melting ice, sitting on fluffy snow - perfect conditions for these same sheets of ice on top of fluffy snow to blow off the tops of transport trucks. This particular morning, I got to meet one close-up.

I was in the passing lane on the Queensway, nearing Kanata (I'd moved to another community south of Ottawa called Barrhaven), in heavy slush conditions, trying to pass a bunch of transport trucks. Pieces of ice were flying off the tops of trucks, when all of a sudden, the entire ice-sheet from the top of a trailer 100 feet in front of me blew off. Through the slush spraying onto my windshield from the tractor-trailer I was trying to pass, I saw the ice-sheet lazily float up, slowly spin, and then drift down, heading straight for me. I was screwed. Just prior to impact, I ducked down as far a possible. WHAM! The ice-sheet took out my entire windshield and miraculously passed over my head into the back seat. Shaking glass off me, I sat up and was treated to an intense 60 mph slush-spray to my face. Thankfully, I was able to hold my hand up enough to block the slush so I could get over onto the shoulder without dying. What a nightmare!

I got the window repaired, and after that, really didn't experience any more "good" car stories. Probably a good thing, eh?

Story #115: Bees and Motorcycles

OK - so maybe I have a motorcycle story. As you, the astute reader may have guessed, the day I left home I bought a motorcycle, having been forbidden by my father to buy one whilst living under his roof.

I loved the thing and drove it continuously, and naturally this included to and from soccer matches. Unfortunately, I discovered that there are problems with wearing loose soccer shorts, and driving a motorcycle. Beyond the nasty discovery that at 60 mph sand, june-bugs, and rain drops really sting, there was the also the problem of my shorts catching bugs. I witnessed this in the worst possible way as I was driving home and caught a bee in my shorts as I was approaching a stop-sign. Now on a motorcycle, all hands and feet are occupied when braking, and as a result I had no choice other than to just let its stinger sink into my upper thigh and deliver a nice, slow, sting. Aaaah! I feel sick just writing this . . .

Appendix C: Bert and Bernard

This appendix is devoted to my Dad's twin cousins on his father's side: Bert and Bernard R. My uncle and my Dad told so many quality stories associated with these two guys, that I was inspired to create an Appendix devoted to them. Bernard was married with kids, but his twin brother was single and lived close by.

As my father puts it - "Misfortune stalked them relentlessly". For instance, one time they came home and found their neighbor dead in their bathroom. He had apparently stopped in to use it while working his nearby field and then had a heart attack.

Story #116: The Horse and the Roof

One day after church in the winter, my father's family decided to stop by Bernard's for Sunday lunch (a regular occurrence, which due to the lack of phones, cell phones, etc. led to suddenly having to double or triple lunch upon spotting relatives showing up unannounced in your lane). Unfortunately for Bert and Bernard, they were preoccupied with trying to figure out how to free a horse from the roof of a wooden shed. Apparently, in the morning, it had climbed up a hard-packed snow-drift onto the roof of one of their sheds, which it promptly fell through.

Story #117: The Tractor and The Well

Another time, stopping by for lunch after church, my father's family pulled into Bernard's lane and found their John Deere tractor with it's front wheels down the well. Apparently Bernard's daughter was learning to drive and

had driven the tractor into the well, and now they were trying to figure out how to pull it out.

Story #118: The Dishwasher

Bernard and his wife Mildred had been saving for a while for a dishwasher, and upon finally getting enough money together, they piled into their pickup truck and headed to the Sears in Saskatoon. Upon buying their dishwasher, they loaded it into the back of their pickup and headed home. Unfortunately, they didn't tie it down, and as luck would have it, they hit a bump just as a transport was passing them, heading the other direction. As Bernard told it, he checked the rear view mirror, and "God damn it - I saw it floating over the back of the truck gate, and then it hit the road and disintegrated." They never bought another dishwasher.

Story #119: Harvest

One time my uncle was helping Bernard with his wheat harvest, and when driving to town in a 2 ton truck full of wheat, they began approaching Highway 16 from a grid road. About half a mile from highway, Garry noticed Bernard starting to shut off the truck engine. Asking him why he was doing this, Bernard replied that he didn't have any brakes and had to time the entry to the highway. Though these guys routinely used such techniques as tying the broken doors shut on their old Nash,[†] the "no brakes on the truck" thing wasn't entirely their fault, as they had to back-order the master-cylinder, and harvest couldn't wait. Bernard even had copy of the order to show the police if he got stopped or things went wrong[‡].

[†] An old model of car that had rear doors that opened forward - aka suicide doors.

[‡] This summer my uncle also remembered that the truck had no rear brake lights as the turkeys would eat the wiring.

Story #120: The Baritone

One day I remember going to get my grandfather's baritone from Bernard's house. Upon asking Bernard for the baritone back, he sent one of his sons to get it. I remember following him to a granary and him digging around in the grain until he pulled out the baritone. To this day, I have no idea why it was there. Apparently there is an older story of them storing a tuba in the granary as well, but being unable to find the mouthpiece and then having to pretend to play it in the local band in order to get the free lunch that was provided.

Story #121: Shooting Gophers

I'm putting this in just because I have the picture, but we had a standing offer from Bert and Bernard to go shoot gophers in their pasture, in exchange for all the .22 long rifle ammo we needed. Now this was not exactly the optimal method of pest control, and in fact it was basically useless - except in the form of some sort of bloody revenge, where somehow you can imagine that the gophers miss their now-dead comrades.

Upon hearing about this offer of unlimited shooting, my brother and I went with my Uncle Garry over to Bert and Bernard's farm and loaded up with ammunition. Then we drove my Uncle's 1976 Pontiac Parisienne into the gopher-filled pasture, put the car in first gear, and climbed out the windows onto the roof. In idle, the car slowly trolled itself around the pasture, while we sat on the roof blazing away at the varmints. Every once in a while you'd have to stick your foot in to steer the car away from a fence, but it worked great - the engine sound got the gophers out, and "Blam!" you bagged them.

Incidentally, I was just out at their place a couple of days ago:

Plate 5.11 **Gopher hunting**

Plate 5.12 **Bert's house today**

www.ingramcontent.com/pod-product-compliance
Lightning Source LLC
Chambersburg PA
CBHW071854020426
42331CB00010B/2518